Rebuilding Mo
Urban Reconstruction in a War Zone

Town Planning Review (TPR) Special Studies

Edited at the Department of Civic Design, University of Liverpool, by
PETER BATEY, MOSS MADDEN, DAVID MASSEY and DAVE SHAW

The scope and thematic coverage of this series reflect the interests of **TPR**, focusing on all aspects of town and regional planning and development in countries with advanced industrial economies and in newly emergent industrial states. From the broad fields of theory, policy, practice, implementation and methodology, among the planning interests of the series are: urban regeneration; environmental planning and management; strategic and regional planning; sustainable urban development; rural planning and development; coastal and estuary management; local planning; local government and planning; transport planning; planning history; and urban design. The following volumes are published:

Planning for Cities and Regions in Japan, edited by Philip Shapira, Ian Masser and David W. Edgington
Vol. 1, 1994, 213pp., ISBN 0–85323–248–2

Design Guidelines in American Cities: A Review of Design Policies and Guidance in Five West-Coast Cities by John Punter
Vol. 2, 1998, 224pp., ISBN 0–85323–893–6

Rebuilding Mostar: Urban Reconstruction in a War Zone by John Yarwood and others
Vol. 3, 1998, 160pp., ISBN 0–85323–903–7

Proposals for future volumes in the series are welcome and should be sent to *The Editors, Town Planning Review, Department of Civic Design, The University of Liverpool, Abercromby Square, Liverpool, L69 3BX, UK*

Rebuilding Mostar
Urban Reconstruction in a War Zone

JOHN YARWOOD MBE

Architect & Urban Planner
Formerly Director of Reconstruction, European Union Administration
of Mostar

with contributions by
ANDREAS SEEBACHER
NIELS STRUFE and HEDWIG WOLFRAM

LIVERPOOL UNIVERSITY PRESS

First published 1999 by
LIVERPOOL UNIVERSITY PRESS
Liverpool, L69 3BX

British Library Cataloguing-in-Publication Data
A British Library CIP record is available

0–85323–903–7

Set in Monotype Plantin by
Wilmaset Limited, Birkenhead, Wirral
Printed and bound in the European Union by
The Alden Press in the City of Oxford

Contents

List of Illustrations

(at end of the book)

The author and publishers are grateful to the following for illustrations appearing in this book: **British Military Survey**: no. 1; **Andreas Seebacher**: nos. 5, 6, 11, 14, 23, 24, 25, 26, 27, 44, 45, 46, 56, 57; **Overseas Development Administration**: nos. 52, 55; **Ćiril-Ćiro Raič**: nos. 29, 30, 31, 32, 33, 34, 35, 36, 37, 38; **Demex**: nos. 12, 13, 15, 16, 17, 18, 19, 20, 21, 22, 23; **GTZ**: no. 4; **EUAM**: nos. 2, 3, 7, 8, 9, 10, 28, 39, 40, 41, 42, 43, 47, 48, 49, 50, 51, 53, 54, 58, 59, 60

Foreword

I am delighted to have been asked to write a foreword to Dr John Yarwood's book on the reconstruction of Mostar, in which he played such a major part.

Before the war in Bosnia and Hercegovina, Mostar had been a fully multi-ethnic, multi-confessional city with a very high percentage of mixed marriages. It was also a beautiful city with a mixture of Ottoman and Austro-Hungarian architecture. It was then ravaged by two wars. The first, when the Croats and the Bosniaks (Muslims) fought together defending Mostar against the Serbs from April until early July 1992, and the second the conflict between the Croats and the Bosniaks from May 1993 until February 1994.

Although it was not a civil war in Bosnia, the conflict in Mostar had all the characteristics of a civil war. This was a city which had the largest number of mixed marriages in the former Yugoslavia and at the time of the 1991 census, had a population consisting of 35 per cent Muslim, 34 per cent Croat, 19 per cent Serbs and the remainder Jews and Yugoslavs. These were people who had lived together, gone to school together, worked together and intermarried—killing each other, and the fighting in Mostar was very fierce. Thus the wounds were deep in such a small city where most people knew each other or at least of each other.

At the end of this fighting Mostar was the most destroyed city in Bosnia and totally divided. (The confrontation line had run down the line of the River Neretva, which flows through the centre of Mostar, but there had been a significant Bosniak enclave West of the river.) This division between the Croats and Bosniaks affected every single walk of life—the ruling structures, the administration, the police, the army, the judicial system, currency and freedom of movement.

The Washington Agreement was signed on 16 March 1994, which brought the Federation between the Croat and Bosniak communities in Bosnia and Hercegovina into being. It was decided that Mostar should be administered for a period of time by an international body because it was recognised that Mostar was the most deeply divided city in the Federation, though it was crucial to that Federation. Thus, the EU took on the responsibility of administering Mostar, and Mr Hans Koschnick from Germany, and the former Mayor of Bremen, who was to achieve such remarkable results, over the next two years, was inaugurated as the Administrator of Mostar on 23 July 1994.

The Administrator had wide powers, bestowed on him by an internationally signed Memorandum of Understanding, and essentially he was given the political aim of unifying the city. Among the aims and principles enshrined in the Memorandum of Understanding was to work towards a single, self-sustaining and multi-ethnic administration of the city, to hold democratic elections before the end of the mandate of the EU Administration, to protect human rights, to work towards the return to their homes of all displaced citizens of Mostar and to uphold the national religious and cultural identity of all the people in the area under the EU Administration. Additionally, a fundamental task was to start the reconstruction of the city, which was in ruins, for which the EU granted a budget of some 270 million DM, or over 100 million pounds. Dr John Yarwood was appointed Head of the Reconstruction Department of the EU Administration.

I will not dwell on the political aspects of the EU Administration, as Dr Yarwood's book concentrates on the reconstruction aspects of the city. Suffice to say that, because of some of the aspects I have mentioned, and the different political aspirations and goals of the Croats and the Bosniaks and indeed the International Community, progress, although significant in many fields, has not been as far-reaching or dramatic as we would have hoped. Further, from the very start the EU Administration faced obstruction from certain leaders of the HDZ (the main Croat political party). Thus, from the summer of 1994, the main problems lay in progress on Freedom of Movement, the formation of a unified police force for Mostar, the return of Displaced People and Refugees to their homes and the formation of a unified government and administration for the city of Mostar. Although much has been achieved, and considerable progress made in these fields, further progress is required before Mostar is a really normal city once more.

Additionally, we faced the problem of what I referred to as the climate of fear and intimidation which existed in Mostar, exemplified by nightly shooting, including machine-gun fire, explosions and expelling of people from their apartments in West Mostar (over 80 cases in 1996 alone). There was also the problem of the Serb Army, who were located only some 4 kilometres to the East of Mostar over the mountains, and who regularly shelled Mostar with their artillery on a random basis until the autumn of 1995. (The Hotel Ero, the seat of the EU Administration, was hit by a large shell, but fortunately we suffered no casualties.) There were, indeed, two attempts on the life of Hans Koschnick during his tenure of office.

Against this difficult political backdrop, the work of John Yarwood's Reconstruction Department worked to make progress under his leadership. It must also be borne in mind that because of these political difficulties, virtually every single reconstruction project had a 'political dimension' to it which slowed progress, and in some cases, prevented the achievement of important projects completely. In spite of these difficulties, 270 million DM was committed to projects and spent in a two-and-a-half-year period, changing the face of Mostar from one of enormous destruction to a city where the people, who had suffered so much, at least were able to live in a degree of normality again.

A great deal of credit for this remarkable achievement goes to John Yarwood for his dedicated and sustained efforts over two-and-a-half years, facing enormous obstacles and difficulties. John Yarwood has every reason to be proud of his remarkable contribution towards the reconstruction of Mostar, and of his assistance in enabling the citizens of the city to return to conditions in which they could start living normal lives again. Much still needs to be done in Mostar, and indeed in the whole of Bosnia and Hercegovina, but John Yarwood's work will live on as a testimony to his achievements and to his contribution to this wonderful city of Mostar which has undergone such horrors during the war.

Sir Martin Garrod
Former EU Special Envoy in Mostar

Mostar, 13 September 1998

Preface

This book is about the work of the European Union Administration of Mostar, and in particular the work of the Department of Reconstruction. It was prompted by the fear that a historically significant development project would go unreported, and that lessons to be learnt from it would be forgotten.

The European Union Administration of Mostar (here abbreviated as EUAM) was a visionary experiment, which may emerge as an influential model in future political and development projects elsewhere in the world. In some respects it was a great success but in others rather less so. Some of its defects were built into the conceptual design, so to speak, and some emerged during its life. But, in any event, many valuable lessons could be learned, to the advantage of the Union itself, its member states and the world at large.

This book is primarily about the reconstruction of a war-damaged city, for which the author was the responsible expert. It is a snapshot at a certain moment—namely the EUAM mandate and its immediate aftermath. I left Mostar in February 1997, returning briefly in June. The book was written in the middle of that year. But events are moving fast, and opinions are in need of constant revision. I gather that in the last year or so, much positive progress has been made in the political sphere. Some of the war politicians are being discredited and a modern leadership is emerging. Political culture becomes more civilised, the city continues to be repaired and the economy to improve. In short, there are reasons for cautious optimism.

This is not an academic book. Events are too recent to allow one to write in such a manner, and many source documents are either not available or are embargoed. The book is more akin to eye-witness reportage, with opinions based on experience and judgement as well as observed facts. But in the Mostar atmosphere, every last thing is politicised, and all current judgements can be challenged by those with different perspectives. The reader should take this into account. It is an inevitable weakness, but I am persuaded that contemporary reportage has its own special value.

The book has two tasks. First, it records facts about what was done by the EUAM and also *how* it was done. Second, it appraises the successes and the mistakes, recommending better ideas and pointing out lessons. Some sections were written by other participants, and occasionally they express opinions with which I do not agree. Such differences are not edited out, but I have added my own footnotes identifying and commenting on them.

The human context—the extraordinary atmosphere in which we worked—is a vital part of the story, and to omit mention on this would create an incomplete—indeed, a distorted—picture. For me and for many others, Mostar was the most exciting and haunting period of our lives, and we were all changed by it, for better or worse.

I must acknowledge my gratitude to many people, especially to former colleagues in Mostar: to Hans Koschnick, the EU Administrator; to General Sir Martin Garrod, the EU Chief of Staff (the best boss I ever had), and to all others sent by EU member states; to my local Co-Directors, Borislav Puljić and Rusmir Ćišić and the water company directors, Prof. Dr Mehmet Sarić and Mario Mikulić, as well as their staff; to my own staff in the Reconstruction Department (whose names and roles are listed in an appendix); and to numerous contractors and consultants—particularly Gunther Scharl and Andreas Seebacher of Technisches Hilfswerk. A remarkable spirit of cooperation, respect and ultimately affection emerged, which surpassed anything I had previously experienced, and which was, I am sure, the real key to our success.

I also thank Colonel Murray McCullough (administrative head for the Office of the High Representative in Mostar), who was a very useful liaison man during the period when I was preparing the manuscript at home.

Outside Mostar, I am indebted to the Overseas Development Administration (now the Department for International Development) who sent me there. When I realised how good was the reputation of the ODA amongst the Bosnians, I became proud to be a member of its staff.

Also I must acknowledge the hard work of Anne Evans and Barbara Bostock in preparing the manuscript so skilfully, as well as the effort and faith of the publisher, without whom the book would never have seen the light of day.

Finally, my greatest debt is to my wife and children, who made far more sacrifices than I did, and gave their support to me without reservation. My wife joined me in Mostar in 1996 and our first grandchild was born during our absence.

John Yarwood
Egremont House
Edgmond
Shropshire
England

Chapter 1

Introduction

The purpose of this chapter is fourfold: first, to describe the history of Mostar until recent times; secondly, to describe the events of the wartime; third, to describe the physical damage; and finally, to describe the origins and purpose of the European Union Administration. The author is not an expert on the history and politics of the area, and this account is cursory. Many books are available which treat these matters in depth, but it is probably helpful nonetheless for the general reader to have a short introduction.

Mostar Before the War

Roman remains abound in west Hercegovina, and Christianisation was given impetus by the Council of Salona (now Solin, near Split) in 533, when the diocese of Sarsentium (perhaps at Cim, a suburb of Mostar) was founded. The leadership of the Church was taken by the Franciscans in the Middle Ages. Their position as defenders of the Christians was strengthened as a result of their persecution by the Ottomans in the sixteenth century. By this point, many local people had converted to the faith of the conquerors, and they naturally became a resented elite. This sort of long past conflict is once again much discussed, and now appropriated by politicians to define the identity of the group over which they wish to claim leadership. I was told by some people that the Bishopric was only revived in the early nineteenth century, and strengthened by the Austrians; the Franciscans had been closer to the people than the supposedly Hapsburg bishops, functioning as parish priests for centuries. Others dispute this interpretation, but in any event, there was an obvious running battle between the bishop and the monks, with the latter firmly committed to Croat nationalism.

When the Ottomans took over (1466 to 1468), the river Neretva was already bridged. The now famous Stari Most (Old Bridge) was built in 1566 by the architect Hajruddin, a pupil of Sinan. A typical Ottoman town emerged at this time on both banks of the river, with a bazaar, public baths, *hans*, thirty mosques, seven *medreses*, residential quarters or *mahallas* and fortifications.

From a peak around 1700, the slow decline of the town paralleled that of the Ottoman empire, until the Austro-Hungarians annexed Hercegovina on 5 August 1878. They brought new administrative and legal forms, new layout patterns with larger dimensions, new materials, eclecticism in design, newspapers, railways and modern roads, public lighting, gas, power, waterworks, industry and capitalist forms of organisation, and advanced education, transforming Mostar from an oriental backwater into a European city in a very few years.

The Austrians intervened in the Ottoman city by creating various individual buildings and one main highway, but the Ottoman form and character remained largely intact. The new quarters were entirely to the west. A neo-classical layout focused on a *rondo*, designed by Miloš Komadina. A smaller intervention on the east bank was Musala Square, with the Hotel Neretva and public baths (both in a Moorish style), as well as the music school.

The Turkish authorities encouraged the creation of Christian churches of both Orthodox and Catholic sects. The church of St Peter and St Paul was completed in 1866. The Orthodox Cathedral—a baroque revival masterpiece, designed by Andrej Damjanovic, and completed in 1873—was financed by the Sultan. The Austro-Hungarians had a similar regard for Islam. For example, Arabic was taught in their schools on the same basis as Latin and Greek. Many of the major buildings were in a Moorish or Islamic style.

The period between the two world wars—the Kingdom of Serbs, Croats and Slovenes and then the Kingdom of Yugoslavia—was stagnant as regards urban development. In the Tito period, after an unpromising start, relatively good residential tower blocks were built in large numbers to the west and north of the Austrian and Ottoman cities. There are a few particularly fine modern buildings, including the Hotel Ruža, designed by Zlatko Uglen and completed in 1978. He had been a pupil of Le Corbusier and the influence is clear. Further west are large low-density suburbs of two-storey villas in big gardens. To the north and south extremities lie large industrial areas which began in the 1950s and 1960s. For example, the Soko plant made aircraft components, Herzegovina Auto made cars, Unis made computers, and also there were large aluminium, wine, tobacco, joinery and food processing factories.

The city lies in a bowl formed by the Neretva and its tributary the Radebolje. This massive amphitheatre is formed by high and steep-sided mountains, interrupted only by the river valleys themselves. It is one of the most dramatic physical settings for a city to be found in Europe. The great periods of building wisely tended to leave work of the earlier times well alone, so that around the river is a delightful zone of predominantly Ottoman character, with later interpolations enriching but rarely intruding. The bright green river, cut deep into the rock, with buildings clustered on its rim; bridge after bridge, culminating in Hajruddin's masterpiece; domes and minarets rising above the sea of red-tiled roofs; and immediately behind, the great mountainsides—all this still forms a great townscape.

According to the 1991 census, the population of the whole municipality before the war was 126 067 persons, of whom 83 686 were concentrated in the city and suburban villages. A further 7812 persons had lived within the EUAM mandate boundary. The urban population was divided into 29 per cent Croats, 34 per cent Muslims, 19 per cent Serbs, 15 per cent Yugoslavs and three per cent other groups. The different groups were spread fairly evenly over the urban area. Only in the

Donja Mahala community did the Muslims constitute 60 per cent, and only in Zahum did the Croats match that proportion (although they formed the great majority in the nearby villages to the west and south). There were no ethnic ghettos in the city. It was a melting pot, with about one-third of marriages being mixed. Many people told me that they never paid attention to ethnicity, and that friendship easily crossed such boundaries. All educational institutions were fully integrated and education reached a high level. Mostar University was well regarded, and Mostar Grammar School was as good as any in Europe. Bosnia (and perhaps Mostar in particular) was held up by the local elite and by visitors alike as a paradigm of a harmonious multi-ethnic society, modern, sophisticated and agreeable. For all practical purposes, it was non-religious (although for several decades religion had been tolerated), and religion was therefore not a source of conflict.

There were 43 866 workers in the city, of whom 17 071 were employed in industry, 3833 in construction, 4204 in trade, 2302 in financial services, and 1626 in craftwork. There were 1784 persons recorded as employed in tourism, but that underestimates by far the significance of the economic contribution made by that industry. There were 70 000 visitors and 120 000 bed-nights spent in Mostar each year in the late 1980s.

Mostar During and After the War

The first war began on 4 April 1992, when Serbian and Montenegrin elements of the Yugoslav National Army (JNA) attacked the city with heavy artillery and multiple rocket launchers. The defence was undertaken by the Croats and Moslems together and the great majority of Serbs fled. The bombardment lasted until June, at which point the Serbs and Montenegrins withdrew for tactical reasons, but only to the nearby mountain tops.

The book *Urbicid*, recording the position in 1992, was written by Croats and Moslems together, and conveys the sense of solidarity which many leading people felt at that time. Krešimir Sego wrote as follows (and this reflection of Croat-Moslem solidarity was typical):

> The architectural manuscript of Mostar expresses an encounter of civilisations, into which the roads from the west and the east, from the north and the south were flowing. Islam and Christianity met here, achieving harmony without imposing it. Thousands of shells were fired into this harmony from all kinds of weapons, a knife cut into it ... with one single aim of exterminating the Croatian and Moslem being.[1]

It is interesting to consider whether the Moslems at this stage had a separate national identity. Foreign scholars have argued that recently they regarded themselves simply as Serbs or Croats, whose ancestors had had a different religion. In 1974, Tito altered the constitution, allowing them to claim the 'nationality' of Muslims. In the early years of this century, efforts were made to assert a Muslim identity, as Pinson has made clear.[2] Some contemporary Moslem politicians, such as Alija Izetbegović, did indeed argue for an enhanced Muslim identity in the period of chaos leading up to the war, but at the time this was a weak affair. The contemporary Moslem identity was forged as a defence against attack.

After the wars, in August 1994, there were said by the Department of Work, Welfare and Family of west Mostar to be 38 475 residents plus 11 245 displaced and expelled persons. Seventy-eight per cent of these displaced persons were living in abandoned dwellings and 16 per cent with relatives or friends. In 1994, the population in the west was claimed to be 78 per cent Croat, 16 per cent Moslem and four per cent Serb. The west urban population was therefore 49 722 persons compared with 51 110 in 1991. A few dwellings—particularly in Podhum—were destroyed, but there was little consequent overcrowding.

In east Mostar, the resident population in August 1994 was said by the Department of Refugees and Displaced Persons to be 20 308 persons. The displaced and expelled were said to number 31 072. In 1991, the population was 24 695 compared with 51 380 now. Bearing in mind the level of structural damage, this suggests serious overcrowding, which was indeed the case.

But these figures are unreliable, and indeed the EUAM conducted its own sample census which told a rather different story. However, because of its sensitivity, it was decided not to make the results public. The gist was that the humanitarian situation was not quite as bad as had been implied. Gunmen continued to expel Moslems from the west side during the EUAM mandate, combining 'patriotism' with profit! We made a determined stand against this, and we had considerable success in containing and reducing such expulsions.

One year after the Serb withdrawal, beginning on 9 May 1993, their erstwhile comrades turned on the Moslems, rounding them up at gunpoint in the middle of the night, assembling them in detention camps, putting them on buses to leave the area, or subsequently expelling them to the ghetto on the east side, which they then bombarded from previously prepared artillery positions. The Muslim population was surprised and obviously unprepared. They had no army, and indeed the JNA had contained very few Moslem officers. Nonetheless, a rag-tag citizens' army made a stand in the east, and despite their overwhelming superiority in men, materials and positions, the Croats were unable to defeat it. The war was a close-fought affair, street by street, building by building. The Croat army used its Moslem civilian prisoners as a human shield in their trenches.

The Moslems were starving, without power or water, living in the cellars of ruined buildings, and emerging at night when the snipers could not see them. It was reported that some snipers were mercenaries, and some of them British. About 2000 people were killed (although doctors, working in appalling conditions on the east side, performed 600 operations with little equipment and few drugs.) Under UNPROFOR protection, a large UNHCR food convoy broke the siege. It was led by a retired British General, the late Jerry Hume. He was a most remarkable character, soldier, statesman and scholar, who became deservedly a hero in the east.

He led UNHCR in Mostar for a further two years, before falling fatally ill. The east side erected a monument to his memory at the east end of Carinski bridge, in front of the railway station.

Croat leaders to whom I talked said that, with the Serbs gone, the Muslim population in the Mostar region formed the majority, and if the Sarajevo government had got a grip on the country, then the Croats would be obliged to abandon the city. It was, they said, their only city, and if they lost it, their community would not be viable. This line was sold to the people, so that even the intelligent started to wonder if it could be true. The Moslems for their part were shocked by the perfidy of their neighbours, colleagues and supposed friends.

The Croats are widely regarded as the guilty party in this affair, but it is necessary to understand their position and avoid simplistic moralising. The Moslem side did commit evil acts in other cities, and the Croats had reason not to trust them. The fear of losing crucial territory was sincerely felt by many people. Over the last hundred years, the Croat nationalist movement had never died, although it had been forced underground (except for the Pavelić regime). It took on a harsh, fascist nature, and when the EU Administrator first arrived in Mostar, he was (as a German) met by Nazi salutes from a few passers-by. There was no irony intended in this, for some people believed that Germany had come to rescue them again. One Croat friend of mine said to me in 1994 that he was proud that his uncle's father had fought and died for the Nazis at the battle of Stalingrad.

This was regrettable, since otherwise nationalism *per se* is not unacceptable, and the modern history of many countries—Finland and Norway for example—is rooted in such feeling. When nationalist conspirators created the para-state known as the Croat Republic of Herceg-Bosna, many were undoubtedly sincere, although a few struck me as mad, and others were mafiosi intent on exploiting chaos to become rich and powerful. The mafiosi on all sides have always cooperated with each other in secret, whilst publicly mouthing nationalist sentiments. Money is a great unifier, and unity will come when the profit margin justifies it.

Given a determined stance by the west, this growth of separatist feeling could have been stemmed. But what happened, happened. And now it is too late to put the genie back into the bottle. We have to make the most of the situation as it stands.

Urban Damage

By 1994 it was clear that much of the city had suffered little damage, but where the damage had been caused, it was severe. The area of the greatest destruction comprised the whole of Muslim east Mostar. To this should be added the eastern part of Podhum, along with buildings on the Croat side of the confrontation line, such as the Privredna Bank building, the Hit Department Store (badly burnt in the first war), and housing along Alexa Santiča Street and Ricina Street. Behind this line serious damage was limited to a few individual buildings, such as the Bishop's Palace. Relatively few buildings on the Croat side had to be totally abandoned. The grammar school was slightly damaged but a few metres away, on the Muslim side of the line, there was a scene of utter devastation. This lack of symmetry reflects the shortcomings of Muslim fire power, I presume.

To give examples from the EUAM damage survey: Brankovac community had 87 per cent of its buildings damaged, with 22 per cent in the heavy category (ruined) and 25 per cent in the medium category. The repair cost for the 1499 damaged structures was computed at DM43.26 million (excluding historic monuments). Likewise, Luka 1 community had 86 per cent of its buildings damaged, with 35 per cent in the heavy (ruined) category and 21 per cent in the medium category. The repair cost for its 858 damaged structures was computed at DM32.95 million.

We may compare this representative picture from east Mostar with a typical situation in the west. In the Rondo community, 55 per cent of the buildings were damaged, with 49 per cent in the light category, four in the medium and two per cent in the heavy. The total cost for repair was DM980 000. In the Avenija community, 34 per cent of buildings were in the light damage category, 4 per cent in the medium category, and none in the heavy category. The computed repair cost was DM3.17 million. Within the urban zone, the east had sustained over four-fifths of heavy damage, as measured by repair costs.

Beyond the urban area, all of the outlying villages in the valley of the Neretva and the eastern hills had sustained very heavy damage, although the villages in the direction of Grude, including Cim, Ilići and Vihovići were little affected. In the case of many villages, the damage did not result from fighting but from the planting of explosives after their residents had been expelled at gunpoint. One favourite method involved the use of butane gas cylinders. Whole villages were utterly ruined in this way. Some buildings were reported to have been destroyed by arson by fleeing Serbs, for example, the Hotel Neretva.

The view is widespread that historic monuments, cultural property and religious buildings were deliberately targeted. On 9 May 1992, the Church of St Peter and St Paul was heavily shelled and completely ruined. On 6 May the Bishop's Palace was destroyed, with its great library of 50 000 books, as was the modern Catholic cathedral. The Serbs again shelled the cathedral at Easter 1995, during the EUAM mandate, killing a group of children. Other lesser churches were destroyed as well, and almost all the mosques were hit. The famous minaret of the Koski Mehmet Paša mosque was felled, destroying one of the most famous urban vistas in Mostar. In revenge, the exquisite Orthodox cathedral was so comprehensively dynamited that not a wall remained. Virtually all historic buildings were severely damaged, to the point of ruination, such as the old Austrian Command Building, the Austrian baths and the Ottoman baths, the Vakufski Dvor, the entire bazaar, the Symphony Orchestra Building, the Museum of Hercegovina and the fortifications of the Old Bridge (the Halebinovka Tower and the Tara Tower).

Bridges have a particular cultural meaning in Mostar—apart from their obvious economic and military significance. Nine were dynamited by the JNA between 24

May and 12 June 1992. The Old Bridge itself survived the first war, but was brought down by Croat tank shells in the second war (during November 1993). At that point, no bridges remained. Subsequently the EUAM rebuilt five of the ten bridges.

Industry was also deliberately and comprehensively looted and dynamited or shelled. All grain silos, mills and bakeries were destroyed in order to disrupt the food supply. The aluminum plant, the Soko aircraft factory, the Hercegovina auto plant, the Hepok wine factory, cotton and tobacco factories, and all buses and public vehicles were heavily damaged and all manufacturing equipment was removed.

The hydro-electric power plant and dam were disabled. Transformers at Ćule, Rodoć, Opine and Raštani were comprehensively destroyed. The Studenac well field was disabled, and the Serbs continued to shell it during the EUAM mandate, hampering but not defeating our efforts to repair it. (At the same time, the Serbs occasionally shelled the Hotel Ero, which was the seat of the EUAM. This ended with the Dayton Agreement.) The telecommunications building was attacked and installations were disabled.

The repair costs estimated by our damage survey are not completely reliable, since they were computed on the basis of standard assumptions. The total estimate for the damaged urban core was almost DM400 million, but this excluded the new industrial estates, the nearby villages and all historic monuments. If these costs were included, then the estimated repair cost would have doubled.

The European Union Administration

The European Union Administration of Mostar (EUAM) was envisaged by the Washington Agreement. It was to be an important instrument in the political stabilisation process in Bosnia. The objectives and constitution were defined in general terms by the Memorandum of Agreement (MOU), signed by representatives of the parties in Geneva on 5 May 1994. This key document provided, in effect, the terms of reference of the EUAM. Our agreed goals included the creation of a unified police force (led by the West European Union); freedom of movement across the front line and public security for all; the establishment of conditions suitable for the return of refugees and displaced persons to their original homes; the establishment of a democratically elected council for a single unified city; and the reconstruction of the buildings and infrastructure as well as the reactivation of public services.

An advance party was sent by the European Union as soon as the MOU was signed. Germany was EU President at that time, and the German Government appointed Hans Koschnick (former Mayor of Bremen) to be the Administrator and H. E. Klaus Metscher as Diplomatic Adviser. The British Government sent Sir Martin Garrod, formerly Commandant of the Royal Marines, as Chief of Staff. The advance party based itself at the Hotel Kaktus in Čitluk, a small town near Mostar in the Croat sector. From here they entered Mostar, and in discussion with local leaders, devised detailed arrangements.

The MOU provided that the Administrator would be the supreme authority in the city (for which a boundary, known as the 'Blue Line', was defined). He was empowered to rule by decree for the period of the mandate, which lasted from 23 July 1994 until 23 July 1996. He was to appoint an 'Advisory Council' representing Croats, Muslims, Serbs, Jews and Yugoslavs (that is to say, those not wishing to identify with other groups). He was bound to report to them and consult them, but no more than that.

The MOU envisaged the establishment of several departments, such as police, education, health and social services, economy, finance and taxation, and reconstruction. Each departmental director would be supplied by an EU member state, and the British sent me to head the Reconstruction Department. Each director would have two co-directors, nominated by the Croat and Muslim sides. My co-directors were Borislav Puljić (formerly City Architect and now Deputy Mayor) for the Croats and Ekrem Sandžaktar, succeeded by Faruk Dizdarević and then Rusmir Ćisić (Deputy Mayor) for the Muslims.

I arrived on 1 September 1994 during a period of lovely autumnal sunshine. I was collected at Split aerodrome by Douglas Houston, the senior Overseas Development Administration (ODA) representative, and driven via Metković to Mostar. I had previously worked in several third-world cities, and had spent the previous year planning the post-earthquake rehabilitation of two cities in the Philippines, but nothing prepared me for the horrific destruction of the towns of the Neretva valley, and Mostar most of all.

The EUAM had taken over and repaired the Hotel Ero, situated on the confrontation line, which remained its seat throughout. We lived and worked there, although as the staff levels grew, an office annex was taken over and some of us moved out into apartments. The Bosnian Serb army was on the mountains overlooking the city and shelled it every day at first. In the streets there was no war but also no peace, and the nights were punctuated by gunfire.

I found everyone at the Ero to be in high spirits, although understandably awestruck by the mission. I was told that two weeks hence the so-called 'Ad Hoc Group on Former Yugoslavia' would meet in Mostar, and I was asked to present my proposals to them. I therefore tried to meet as many local people as possible and to visit all parts of the city. I had three translator/secretaries allocated to me, but no technical staff. My conclusion was that I should set up five sections in my department, namely:

- Building Repair and Demolition;
- Infrastructure Repair;
- Construction Industry Revival;
- Urban Planning; and
- Administration, Contracts and Finance.

The budget for the remainder of 1994 (as well as the whole budget) was known. I was able to take a view on the immediate priorities and guess the rough allocation of resources. Experience allowed me to deduce the number of project management staff needed to expend certain amounts of money for each purpose. I proposed therefore that member states supply a deputy director for each of the five sections; that a total department of thirty staff was needed (to be recruited locally) but that external consultants be retained for selected specialised tasks.

The Ad Hoc Group, comprising diplomats from each member state and chaired by Michael Steiner, met in the Hotel Ero on 14 September. At the appropriate time, I presented my provisional programme of investment and the principles behind it, and I then asked for the staff. Everything was accepted, except the size of the department, which was seen as extravagantly large. It became obvious that no one had the slightest idea about the scale of practical effort which the budget implied. Required by Mr Koschnick to achieve concrete results with no delay, I pressed ahead without staff for four months. The results were there, but project control was non-existent and the scope for error or corruption was eventually obvious to all. I was then allowed to appoint staff and by early 1995 a competent departmental team had been set up.

NOTES

1 Šego Krešimir (ed.), *Urbicid Mostar 92*, Mostar, 1992, p. 24.
2 Pinson, Mark, 'The Muslims of Bosnia-Hercegovina under Austro-Hungarian Rule' in Pinson, Mark (ed.), *The Muslims of Bosnia-Hercegovina*, Cambridge, MA, Harvard UP, 1994.

Chapter 2

The Human Factor

This chapter will try to evoke a little of the working environment—the atmosphere, the culture, and the practical circumstances. Every organisation has such an environment—democratic, charismatic, creative, dull, hostile, cohesive, or whatever—and the product of the organisation is heavily conditioned by it. Context must be considered in order to grasp a true picture and draw reliable conclusions.

The Atmosphere

I have never known such an extraordinary atmosphere as that which developed in and around the EUAM. It arose, I think, from eight factors.

- The historic gravity of the mission: we felt that we had been given an awesome and perhaps impossible task, upon which the future of an entire country and even ultimately the well-being of the continent might depend (or so it seemed at the time).
- The scale of effort required: both the task and the budget were very big. The staff levels at the outset were low, but the pressure to urgently achieve results was high. This led to sustained overwork.
- Exposure to the eyes of the world: for the first year, Mostar was subject to intense scrutiny by the governments and media of many countries.
- A sense of isolation, lack of precedents and a degree of independence of action: notwithstanding our exposure, we had delegated from the Council of Ministers a very high degree of freedom of action. Within the EUAM itself, departmental directors were left to make their own decisions to a great extent. No one told us what we should be doing, as they knew that even less than we did ourselves. There were no precedents and no prior experience on which to decide what action to take. Even on normal bureaucratic matters, the European Commission provided us with no rules.
- A sense of physical danger: actual shelling and street violence were allied to a fear of direct attacks, against which we were practically defenceless.
- The devastation of the city: the environment was a constant and tragic reminder of human stupidity, and the continuing actions of politicians

and hooligans reinforced the need to continue the struggle against a moral vacuum.

- The absence of a local system: there were no obviously legitimate local political and administrative institutions, and often we could not tell who held power and responsibility. There were no effective courts and the applicability of laws was obscure.
- Strong leadership: Mr Koschnick provided charismatic leadership. Sir Martin Garrod was an inspiration—calm and steady, optimistic, good natured and totally competent. With such leaders, the team kept its head and developed a sense of unity in spite of all difficulties.

To sum up, we had a sense of the gravity and exposure of our position, but felt disorientated and isolated. To work in this milieu and so intensely with colleagues produced in the end a sense of belonging, loyalty and brotherhood. The main point is, of course, that it could easily have ended in disaster. The common vices of jealousy, in-fighting and backstabbing could easily run out of control in such a superheated atmosphere, and end by destroying the vigour of the team. Apart from a few shocking moments, this did not happen. Steady comrades are needed if you paddle up the Amazon in a small canoe, and internal strife will only benefit the alligators.

We came through to the end with a great sense of pride in a shared achievement. When my department closed, and we said goodbye, some tears were shed. Early leavers kept up their visits as if we had been a family, and bonds were forged which I am sure will never break.

Building Local Relationships

It was obvious from the start that the most important factor in our success would be the creation of an appropriate relationship with the local technical elite, who were found mainly in the municipalities or linked to them. We were reliant on their cooperation to get things done. The scope for resentment, misunderstanding and obstruction was much greater than I had found in other foreign projects. No amount of technical skill would compensate for bad human relations. In the event, we succeeded in creating outstandingly good relationships; I feel this was the real achievement, next to which the technicalities (discussed later in this book) take second place: that was the easy bit.

In this type of work, one needs to balance empathy and propriety. The locals deserved respect: I found them to be professionally sound, energetic and sincere—with a few exceptions. I tried to see situations from their point of view. How would I feel if I were in their shoes? What would I be asking the EUAM to do? What would be my bottom line? I reminded myself that they had in many ways more knowledge, more insight and more control over events than we had. Moreover, this was *their* country and their city, whereas I was a visitor—here today and gone tomorrow.

I therefore began by showing that I respected them as people and that I respected their community and its identity. I did not make the mistake of feeling sorry for them, nor did I see myself or my employer as a charitable agency: this would lead to a false sense of superiority, to condescension and mutual resentment. I assumed I was there purely as a professional man to do a technical job (in exchange for a good salary). The task of rebuilding Mostar was *their* task, and the EUAM would not try to expropriate that. Our wish was to support and strengthen their capability. This meant a corporate style based on open teamwork, sharing, and insightful compromise. I therefore did a lot of listening and tried by words and body language to communicate my respect and responsiveness. On the other hand, we also had to communicate the EU's bottom line. It seemed that this had two component parts. First, we had to create a sound administrative framework, particularly regarding project identification and contractual as well as financial matters, so that the European taxpayer's money was honestly and wisely spent. Second, we had to use every opportunity to reinforce the political aims of the Memorandum of Understanding, subject to overriding humanitarian needs and sensible pragmatism.

Political theories were all very well, but technical progress would emerge from a real-world, commonsense recognition that one must work creatively within the limits of what cannot be immediately changed. Given that, we would achieve progress from small incremental improvements upwards, and should not try to impose grand political schemes from the top down. This philosophy struck my local colleagues as wholly reasonable. I often asked them, during arguments, what they would do if they were in my position: the answer was always that they would do what I was proposing.

I think that this philosophy worked well. Local colleagues seized the opportunity to take the initiative and this released a lot of optimism, energy and pride. On the other hand, they responded to directions without sustained opposition, because they always saw the logic of the position, and also because I never tried to force them suddenly to cross their own bottom line. They knew that I had always delivered the results they wanted and so they, for their part, did the same for me.

I came to like the Bosnians very much. Sadly, a few EU colleagues came to detest them. We were like psychotherapists, helping people to cure their own problem. Why would a psychotherapist storm out in anger just because the patient was apparently mad? The Bosnians are not mad. My colleagues were all good people trapped in a nightmare. But, in any case, even mad people have their *own logic*, and you can only direct them within the framework of *that* logic, whilst trying all the time to change it. But the speed of such change—whether fast or slow—must be organic with the reality intrinsic to *their* situation—not yours.

The Hotel Ero

The Hotel Ero played a major part in the life of the EUAM and took on a symbolic role for everyone in Mostar. We lived in bedrooms on the upper storeys and our offices were on the lower floors. Countless meetings—whether humble technical committees or high-level political negotiations—were held in the meeting rooms. The dining room, bar and foyer flowed together into one space, which linked out to an external dining terrace, and this was constantly full of soldiers, diplomats and politicians of all nations, secretaries, contractors, bureaucrats, engineers, citizens, and gangsters coming and going, talking, dining, drinking, embracing, arguing, and occasionally singing and fighting. There were orchestral concerts, exhibitions, receptions, dances and parties.

The Refugee Adviser, H. E. Bo Kaelfors, said that he believed he had walked into the film *Casablanca*, and soon signs appeared saying 'Rick's Bar'. The Ero, being the seat of the European Union, on the confrontation line, with guaranteed access to all people without restriction, immediately became a beacon of hope for ordinary people.

Having such a home made an impact upon the culture of the EUAM. This became apparent when other organisations later moved to Sarajevo, and set up normal offices, such as may be found in any city, from which tired workers trudge home to their apartments at five o'clock. These organisations were typical of the kind of normal bureaucracy that can be found the world over. The Ero drew people like a light draws moths. It kept most of us at work seven days a week until late at night, condensing and expressing the mission and obliging us to hold fast to it.

Incidents

Various incidents also created a history and corporate mythology. I will recall several. Just after midnight on 11/12 September 1994, several misfits fired a rocket-propelled grenade at Mr Koschnick's bedroom. Fortunately we were finishing dinner on the terrace at the time, or else he would have been killed and the mission would have been aborted by an already nervous German government.

Two days after the attack, Mr Koschnick opened the Musala Bridge. This spanned the River Neretva in the centre of the city. It had been destroyed by the Serbs in the first war, and was now rebuilt by the Royal Engineers using a 'Bailey Bridge' financed by the ODA. It was the first major project of the mandate, and had obvious symbolic power. Bridge-building was a fashionable metaphor at that time. The bridge connected the Muslim west bank to their east bank foothold. Some Croats saw this as having military significance. They were not happy. At the time, no one knew what lay behind the attack on Koschnick's bedroom. The question now arose as to whether a major public opening ceremony was an invitation to extremists to instigate a bloodbath. Koschnick would not consider such cautious counsels, and so the ceremony went ahead.

A large party gathered in the Hotel Ero, including a lot of foreign journalists. We walked along the rubble-strewn Kolodvorska Street and turned left. The bridge lay ahead, surrounded by row upon row of ruined buildings. Small knots of citizens applauded politely. Koschnick and General Ridgeway led the large but silent procession. Koschnick stood on a small podium on the terrace of the former Hotel Bristol, next to the river. He delivered a short speech on the theme of bridge-building. The mood was tense. On top of the ruins were sandbagged machine-gun nests. Our position was nonetheless completely exposed. A sniper could have hit the Administrator, and the Serbian artillery, located on nearby mountain tops, could have landed shells very close.

Nothing happened. After the speech, Koschnick cut a ribbon and we all crossed the bridge. The mood now became more relaxed. For my part, I felt that this was a historic event—the only one which I had witnessed in my life. I was deeply struck by Koschnick's courage and strong will.

At that time the city was littered with street barricades. The largest was outside the Ero itself. It consisted of heavy lorries piled with sandbags, steel sheets and assorted rubbish. It faced east across the blown Carinski Bridge. Koschnick was affronted and determined to get rid of it. He ordered the Croats to remove it, but they refused. In those brave days, it was our policy to ask for something politely three times, and then to act alone. We got our three refusals, so Koschnick asked UNPROFOR for engineers to remove the offending article.

I was working in my office at midnight the same day. At that time my office was located on the first floor on the street corner. Suddenly the sky outside the window lit up and I heard a tremendous roar. I rushed on to the balcony. The intersection was brilliantly floodlit. Heavy cranes, bulldozers and shovels were arriving and soldiers guarded the area from rooftops. General Ridgeway had ordered his engineers to drive from Gornji Vakuf to Mostar to do the job. The machines were moving in a small compass at high speed with complete precision. The surprise and speed were presumably necessary to minimise the risk of retaliation.

A bewildered local crowd gathered. Everyone rushed out of the hotel. Then a soldier had the idea of putting diesel into one of the wrecked lorries. He succeeded in starting it and drove it away, scattering the sandbags and other rubbish in all directions. The Croats were furious and said this barricade was essential from their military standpoint. After a few days, however, the *fait accompli* was history and was not mentioned again. Soon after, all the other barricades came down.

There was a tense time during negotiations for prisoner exchange. A Croat prisoner had been plausibly accused of raping two young Muslim girls and was reported to be a hardened criminal. However, he was also some sort of chieftain. The Muslims refused to hand him over and a rag-tag army (with a tank) assembled on the edge of Mostar, promising to attack the Ero and enter east Mostar in order to take him back by force. Mr Koschnick helped to instigate talks between both sides in the hotel. It was his policy that the Ero should be a public place. Anyone could come

THE HUMAN FACTOR   15

in. During the talks, the hotel foyer and bar filled with hoodlums. Happily, the talks succeeded, but it was an anxious day.

Armed extremists celebrated the birthday of Adolf Hitler in the dining room of the Ero, becoming very drunk and singing fascist songs. This was a typical provocation which distressed us all. The Legal Adviser, a Swiss, had the courage to object. A fight was narrowly avoided.

The most fateful event of all was undoubtedly the attempt to sack the hotel and murder Mr Koschnick. The events which precipitated a mass protest are described in Chapter 4. A peaceful crowd was joined by no more than twenty known extremists who blocked and attacked Mr Koschnick's car savagely. Local colleagues told me later that these men had guns in their car boots. I was about 20 metres away from the car and heard shots, but fortunately the car was armoured. After an hour or more, the Croat mayor arrived and called on the crowd to disperse. Koschnick drove to the police headquarters. Meanwhile, flags were trampled and songs sung outside the Ero. The hotel was invaded by a small crowd, which trashed the ground floor, but the extremists could not marshall enough support to invade the EU offices. Had they done so, I do not like to imagine what would have happened. Free ice-cream and lemonade were served, which distracted the younger rioters: clearly the average Croat is no extremist.

This event had a considerable political fallout, but that is a story for others to tell. Neither our own police nor the Spanish battalion of IFOR (the Dayton Agreement Implementation Force) were able to intervene to protect their charges. The moral is that one should think twice before attempting a task against sure opposition which one has not the means to even attempt to quell. This is also a matter of timing and the management of the speed of change.

Conclusion

This little bit of historical background illustrates what we were dealing with. Some responded to such events with deep anger and hurt pride. Some, of course, were born cynical, some became cynical and some had cynicism thrust upon them. But others, the pragmatists, refused to give up, learnt the lessons and carried on.

Chapter 3

Organisation

This chapter begins by examining the relationship between the organisation in Brussels and that in Mostar. This was the most fundamental source of success, but also the cause of several shortcomings. This leads on to a consideration of the basic aims and methods of the EUAM (as set out in the so-called 'Memorandum of Understanding'). Then we review the internal organisation of the EUAM as a whole, and that of the Department of Reconstruction in particular. Next the relationship between the EUAM and the local municipal administrations is considered. This is followed by a consideration of the relationship between the political mission and the technical mission. The last section draws some conclusions.

Decision-Making and Financial Control: The Brussels-Mostar Relationship

The key to the practical success of the EUAM was almost complete delegation from Brussels. A single organisation, with a single decision maker—the Administrator—had been established on the ground. The essential objectives were given in the Memorandum of Understanding, signed by the parties before the beginning of the mandate. The financial resources were defined and handed over to the control of the Administrator. The team on the ground, with the Administrator fully in charge, decided everything, and implementation followed at speed. If necessary and appropriate, one could obtain Mr Koschnick's formal approval to a project on Monday, draft a contract on Tuesday and sign it on Wednesday, order payment on Thursday and the money would be transferred by the following Monday.

About 500 contracts were signed, and DM170 million paid in two years on reconstruction projects, starting from a tabula rasa in every respect. It is certain that without delegation, and without professional expertise, little would have been achieved. This arrangement was a revolutionary step for the Union and in particular the Commission. Nothing of the sort had ever occurred before. Normally, all decisions of legal and financial significance—however small—must be taken in Brussels and never at local level. But responsibility in Brussels is divided and the speed of decision-making is slower than the natural pace of events. Also, there are no permanent technical officials in the Directorate-General responsible for Bosnia. At least until early 1997 (when I left) the EC had no expert reconstruction team in theatre, except in Mostar.

This is not to malign generalist administrators but merely to assert the importance of professional training and experience, as well as continuous local presence, when dealing with reconstruction. I observed the practical consequences of this situation, as it applied to the EU operations in Bosnia as a whole. The contrast with Mostar was striking. The EU deserves great praise for the way it set up the EUAM, and in my opinion, the Commission will make progress in Bosnia as a whole only when it applies its 'Mostar model' on a wider scale. Such an approach has six characteristics:

- a multi-disciplinary team of experienced professional experts on the ground;
- a single leader with strong decision-making powers;
- clear strategic task definition and broad rules made explicit by the centre;
- a global budget released at the outset, with money on account;
- power to approve projects, sign contracts and authorise payments delegated to the staff on the ground; and
- the centre to receive reports, monitor/audit and issue timely guidance.

Brussels could have improved operations in Mostar by careful preparation and planning. The first problem was that the Finance Department was not functioning in a mature way for the first few months of reconstruction. The second problem concerned human resources. The international staff were supplied by member states separately, with no central coordination as to job description or person specification. As the EU Court of Auditors noted in its report, it was by luck that an appropriate and harmonious team eventually emerged. Also, local recruitment was long delayed because early ideas envisaged an impractically small establishment. To illustrate this, the Advance Party proposed eight cars, and the EU cut it to five. But after a few months we actually had almost fifty cars!

The point is, of course, that advance planning is vitally important if you want to have a steep learning curve and 'hit the ground running'. The task was entrusted to the Foreign Ministry of the Presidency, but this changes by rotation every six months. Continuity is a problem. Perhaps the answer would have been to establish a small permanent, integrated and expert 'Mostar Unit' to carry full responsibility. The Advance Party in 1994 had sent twenty-eight faxes to Brussels asking for instructions and it never received a single reply. (This is noted in the Court of Auditors' Report.) I was also surprised to find that neither the EU nor the Commission sent any technical missions to monitor our work and give advice. I had previous experience of World Bank expert missions and I reflected that such monitoring would have upgraded the quality of our work, as well as alerting Brussels to the need for action here or there.

The Memorandum of Understanding

One aim of the MOU was to create a unified public administration system for the city. Each department of the EUAM would be led by a West European, but his two 'co-heads' would be Croat and Muslim. The Administrator also had two counterparts, namely the mayors of the Croat and Muslim municipalities.

Key targets included freedom of movement for all citizens across the whole city; a unified police force of both Croats and Bosniaks under the direction of the West European Union; and a single public finance system, including tax and revenue collection, under the direction of the EUAM Department of Finance and Taxes. Although we made repeated, strenuous (and partly successful) efforts to achieve freedom of movement and unified public security, the EUAM never made any attempt to unify public finance, or to place it on a sustainable basis. In fact (notwithstanding the MOU) we concerned ourselves only with internal EU finances. If you believe that discretion is the better part of valour, then this decision might be seen as wise. In any case, it had a major effect on what the Reconstruction Department could achieve as regards sustainable operation of urban systems.

The MOU enabled the Administrator, after consultation with the 'Advisory Council' of prominent local politicians, to issue decrees which had the force of law in perpetuity. Lacking the means to enforce such decrees, of course, the Administrator had to proceed with caution. Decrees relevant to reconstruction included Fiduciary Management of Property with Unclear Ownership, and Demolition of Dangerous Buildings.

The ultimate aim was to hold democratic local elections for a single city council comprising Croats, Muslims and others. The new mayor would then take over from the Administrator and the EUAM apparatus would dissolve itself. This was indeed achieved, but the vision surely implied the creation of an actually-functioning city administration mechanism prior to elections. Had we started to construct this machine in 1994, then we might have succeeded. But we began only in 1996, and even then we concerned ourselves with the outline on paper and never with the practical nitty-gritty. The elections were efficient, and Mostar got its city council and mayor. But it has not got a functioning urban management machine, and at the time of writing (early 1997) still relies upon the two old municipal systems of the divided city.

Advisory Council and Principal Counsellors

One evening every month the Advisory Council met as required by the MOU, with the Diplomatic Advisor, H. E. Klaus Metscher, in the chair. The Administrator, Mr Koschnick, would make a report on progress, events and issues. The two mayors then replied, making their own points. A general discussion ensued and sometimes the meeting lasted until ten o'clock at night. This was followed by a convivial dinner. Conversation—animated but not unfriendly—continued sometimes long into the night. The members were appointed by the Administrator upon the recommendation of one side, and with the agreement of the other. This was an oligarchy, of course, but there was no possible alternative at that stage. I think these meetings were valuable as psychotherapy, and over two years did much to reconcile the former warring parties. On the other hand, they did not function as business meetings. Questions of policy or action were never given clear definition and put forward for decision. This was not an accountable body, and played little role in steering the reconstruction process.

The MOU envisaged the two mayors as the 'Principal Counsellors' of the Administrator, and they met together, usually with respective deputies, every morning. I attended on occasion and I gained the impression that here was the real forum at which ideas were tested and deals were struck. Even here, however, reconstruction strategy was not much discussed.

EUAM Organisational Structure

The details of the internal structure of the EUAM were devised by the Advance Party in early June 1994. It consisted of three elements: departments, advisers and central administration. The departments were:

- City Administration;
- Education;
- Cultural Life, Youth and Sports;
- Health and Social Services;
- Economic Development and Transport;
- Reconstruction;
- Finance and Taxes; and
- Police.

There were advisers for press relations, refugees, humanitarian matters, legal matters, diplomacy and military matters. The internal administration included Chiefs of Logistics, Personnel, Transport etc, as well as a Paymaster. They reported to the Head of Administration. Formally all heads and advisers reported directly to the Administrator, but the Chief of Staff, Sir Martin Garrod, filtered all matters before they reached him. The structure was very flat, nonetheless, with fourteen people reporting directly to the top.

There was no formal process of internal corporate working. There was an occasional 'Heads of Departments Meeting', which mainly dealt with minor administration matters in an *ad hoc* manner. It played no corporate management role, such as brainstorming about strategy or coordinating implementation. Efforts to create a corporate system of committees or task forces did not succeed. It was decided in October 1994, that each head of department was free to set up his own committees if he wanted. The reason, I think, was fear of encroachment by one EU member state or representative upon the freedom of another. This perhaps also explains the need to have fourteen people with equal access to the top.

The idea of a 'corporate plan' was also rejected. The Administrator was persuaded to go along with the idea of a 'Strategy Paper', which was prepared in November 1994. It was then 'put on ice' until March 1995, when it was reviewed at a conference in Neum. It was finally signed by the administrator on 13 May 1995. However, most colleagues were sceptical. The paper was an anthology of departmental contributions. It was never consulted, monitored or reviewed after that. The only corporate document was the budget, which allocated portions of the cake to the various departments.

Division of Responsibilities

In October 1994, it was decided to remove some reconstruction responsibilities from the Reconstruction Department and pass them to other departments. Thus, for example, the Department of Culture, Youth and Sports became responsible for telecommunications; the Economy Department for electricity; the City Administration Department for solid waste collection and disposal; and the Education and Health Departments for building repair in respect of schools and hospitals. Several departments began to employ architects and engineers.

This can be explained quite simply. Most people saw the task of the EUAM only in terms of the repair of physical objects, and specifically buildings and infrastructure. They undervalued other tasks, such as education, culture, public finance or institutional development. Given this perception, it was politically imperative to carve up construction between different departments, so that each member state had a slice of the cake.

I pointed out that a 'client department' could control a budget—for education, say—but a specialist department should execute the technical job. This idea was not understood. Two or three consequences arose. It was quite natural that some colleagues were distracted by the technicalities of construction, in which they were not trained, from fully addressing more vital issues. To take the case of education, for example, problems of insufficient manpower, lack of books and teaching material, curriculum development, teacher training, system finance and staff remuneration were never addressed at all. In early 1997, five schoolchildren were sharing one pre-war book. All the allocated budget was spent on repairing buildings, and in consequence the repair budget (as between, say, schools and housing) became unbalanced.

A second consequence was some degree of non-coordination of technical activity between departments. I commissioned consultants to prepare a coordinated urban infrastructure strategy (between September and November 1994). But by the time it was complete, I controlled only water and sanitation in the sphere of infrastructure.

Other colleagues did not accept this plan, and refused to set up an Infrastructure Coordination Committee. Perhaps they believed the Brits were trying to regain power through the 'back door'! This was not so. One accepted the changes with good grace, having in mind that harmony amongst colleagues was more important than anything else.

The EU Court of Auditors commented upon the somewhat different project management procedures employed by each department. They could not understand why a strictly consistent approach to identical matters was not adopted. However, the engineers and architects working in all departments did an excellent job. The EU should be proud of all of them.

Departmental Staffing and Organisation

I was asked to propose a broad departmental programme to the Ad-Hoc Group on Former Yugoslavia, meeting in Mostar on 14 September 1994. I took the opportunity also to outline a departmental organisation and to request appropriate staff. I proposed five groups, each led by a Deputy Head. The groups proposed were:

- Building Repair;
- Infrastructure;
- Planning;
- Construction Sector Recovery; and
- Project Finance and Administration.

I proposed that member states supply an expert to lead each group. I envisaged their technical staff would be locally-recruited professionals, but that special expertise would be provided by international consultants on a short-term basis. I envisaged a total staff of thirty people, including secretaries and translators. This estimate assumed a fairly 'hands-on' approach. Project managers would, I proposed, direct designers in the preparation of drawings and bills of quantities; organise tendering and analyse bids; set up contracts and check works on site; issue 'variation orders'; check invoices and document payment requests; and so on.

Experience suggested that this would cost a fee-equivalent of two per cent of capital value. From this, given the budget in gross terms, one could calculate the approximate staff requirement. However, at this stage, the EU believed this was too big a department.

After a couple of months it became clear to everyone that we had no grip on projects, and that we would later be accused of maladministration of public funds. Mr Koschnick had wanted immediate action and therefore I forged ahead and committed DM18 million by Christmas, but could not check documents and visit all sites myself alone. I was therefore permitted to advertise for local staff in November, and the department effectively came into existence in February 1995.

I also proposed the extensive use of consultants to prepare strategic plans and undertake specialised work. I believed that immediate action should run in parallel to advance planning during the period September to December 1994, so that we would have a solid base for rational action in 1995. I came under fire for this. It was perceived as a waste of money—mere words, paper, discussion—as opposed to 'action'. Perhaps also some people were not aware of the role and purpose of consultants in development work. I set up exercises such as a building condition survey; an infrastructure survey and action plan; and a construction sector revival strategy. But I was obliged to cancel or curtail this work. As a result, our activity sometimes lacked a really solid foundation: we felt our way forward, taking decisions on the basis of guesswork rather than knowledge, or taking incremental decisions without a strategic framework.

Upgrading of Institutional Management and Finance

A related issue concerned the repair, so to speak, of the institutions and processes of urban management and finance. Through 1994 I argued that money should not be used like opium (which would breed dependency and subsequent withdrawal shock), but rather as a healing drug which would leave a strong and sustainable situation after our departure. In particular, I was worried that the infrastructure companies could not function. They had no trained engineers, no management, no income and no system to collect income. This applied, in principle, of course to other areas as well, such as health care and education, as well as public housing. Ultimately, perhaps, it went to the heart of the public finance system itself.

I argued that after the emergency phase was complete and water was again fully available (which occurred in March 1995), we should have ready a 'Water Company Business Plan'. Our expenditure should support the business plan from then on. I envisaged recruitment of engineers and managers to the water company; creation of a tariff and collection system underpinned by a consumer subsidy (tapering over time), restructuring of company debts; re-equipment and so forth—as well as capital investment in repairs and new works, of course.

It is obvious that some forms of capital investment could increase costs above income, and thereby hasten the demise of the company. This needed proper analysis. Already the water company's debt to the electricity company was massive. It could not pay its workers and they went on strike. The courts gave a judgement to allow assets (financed by the EU) to be seized. We spent DM20 million on physical objects, but the company was not viable. The EUAM position was originally clearly articulated by Mr Koschnick and the Finance Director. They would not use EU money to subsidise operation or to discharge any task which was seen as a normal municipal duty. They would not involve themselves in support of public finance: their task was to repair or replace physical objects.

However, by late 1995, the intellectual climate changed as the water company approached breakdown and Mostar was threatened with a loss of water supply—but this time not due to warfare! I again tried to get agreement to have consultants prepare a business plan, and this time I succeeded. But it was too late to guide EUAM action, because all our funds were committed. However, in 1996 the World Bank started to work in Bosnia, and they proposed the provision of funding to support the plan. I believe there will be a successful outcome, not least because the two sides, Croat and Muslim, are keen to create a viable single company for the whole city.

Time Horizons and the Issue of Continuity

A strict timescale of two years was given by the MOU. The Commission interpreted this to mean that every project must be finished and every man should leave Mostar on or before 23 July 1996. No ideas about EU presence in Mostar after July were discussed until early 1996 and no decisions were taken until August! Then an extension (but without the original mandate) was agreed until December. Again in late December an extension was agreed to June, but then curtailed to April. But reality forced an extension to September. Even staunch supporters of the EC were not impressed.

A two-year time horizon for so complex and ambitious a project was obviously unrealistic. This was recognised by many people at the beginning. We were unable to conceptualise long-term goals for investment. I argued for a small mission to provide training and advice from 1996 to 2000, with few staff and no new capital budget, in order to allow us to follow through the investment phase into a period of consolidation and system development. I think my EU colleagues in Mostar could see the value of this but Brussels did not respond. The inability to think beyond the mandate meant that we lost some of the longer-term benefits which the investment already made could have yielded. We sowed but we did not bother to reap.

Unification of City Administration

At the beginning, Mr Koschnick accepted not a single EU administration, but three separate entities: the EUAM, and the two established municipalities, Croat and Muslim. In the local language, the EU Administration was not 'of' Mostar but 'over' Mostar. This approach was pragmatic and also avoided charges of imperialism: at the time, it seemed a wise decision.

One key aim of the MOU was to unify the city by creating a unified administration. Certainly this meant holding elections for a single council, which was done efficiently. We also produced (and negotiated to acceptance) a city statute. But this was of limited value in practice since there was no actually-functioning administrative machine to advise and support the political committees and execute their decisions. To create such a machine in any situation is time-consuming, but in so bitterly divided a city, it is a special challenge.

The EUAM view was that the administration would be created once the elections were held and the legal statute was adopted. Might it not have been better to create the machinery of city government first? The end of the mandate followed very soon after the elections and left us no time. Much of our power, *de facto*, was also gone, because the money was spent.

In practice we worked in an *ad hoc* manner by building harmonious and efficient teamwork between three distinct entities. In reconstruction, this was quite successful. My co-heads and I decided to set up a Housing Committee, a Water and Sanitation Committee (which ran for two years) and other smaller project committees as needed. Agencies upon which we relied for effective action were represented. Gradually dynamic and harmonious teams developed, based on honesty, openness and creative collaboration.

We provided proper municipal offices, and furniture and equipment of all types. I also insisted on paying fees for professional and managerial work done by municipal organisations to implement our projects, and this gave them working capital and psychological motivation. They recovered self-confidence and hope for the future. All this was good, but nonetheless it strengthened or entrenched both the existing pattern of east-west division and the old oligarchic spirit.

I wrote a short paper in October 1994 proposing a two-tier system of administration. I suggested that the Croat and Bosniak zones retain local administrative entities covering all local matters. But a unified central authority would handle those strategic matters which could only be considered for the whole city. For example, strategic planning and control of infrastructure, broad land use, major projects, economic development, environmental protection etc. would be handled by the upper tier, whereas local planning, development control, maintenance of landscape and construction project management etc. would be handled at the lower tier. Both tiers would constitute a single Technical Agency, however, with a tripartite structure comprising the Strategic Team, the Local Team (West) and Local Team (East). I proposed that the EU staff be integrated into this structure until the end of the mandate, so that the EUAM Reconstruction Department would cease to have a fully independent existence (although we would keep control of allocation and management of EU funds). In the case of the water industry, I proposed a similar tripartite arrangement. Operations and maintenance would be done by local teams, east and west, but planning, design and finance would be unified. The EUAM Water Team would then join the water company until the end of the mandate.

This idea was enthusiastically accepted by the local officials. Even Croat hard-line separatists agreed. For example, one of them said to me, in a memorable phrase, that there was 'only one River Neretva: the water and the pollution is not Croat or Muslim'. Such things must be handled in the common interest together. Hard-liners also agreed that other infrastructure and the broad pattern of land use were incapable of being regulated separately. Both sides wanted the EUAM to become involved in their own administrations, hoping for advice, training, reform and general improvement.

The opposition came from the EU side. I think there were two reasons. We did not trust the locals, and did not accept the idea of sharing ideas, information and influence. Some EU people did not want to be too close to their local counterparts. Second, the EUAM wanted to construct a fully integrated, single tier system, and to negotiate this from the top downwards. We sought (but did not find) high-level political agreement to this global pattern. We intended to look later at detail and function, but were blocked at the earlier stage. An alternative view would be that one should begin from the bottom in a concrete way, and work pragmatically upwards.

I remember finding in the Hotel Ero dining room a slice of onion. It had two cores within a single oval cross-section. Was this unified or divided? I argued that we could build concrete unity only by accepting now some degree of division. Such alternatives were not debated in 1994/95. The EUAM policy remained rather abstract and idealised. When this changed, it was too near the end of the mandate to create a functioning administrative machine.

However, we did make some pragmatic progress. As described later, a unified Urban Planning Team was established, and it produced some good work towards an All-Mostar Structure Plan. The managers and staff of the two water companies worked very warmly and closely together from the early days. We set up a Technical Training Centre where staff from east and west worked together. I saw this as the precursor of unification: if staff could study their subjects together, it would be a short step to actually working on them together.

I think we pointed the way forward. We changed the mentality of local officials. They came to see cooperation as a possibility. Mutual suspicion and fear were significantly eroded.

The Linkage between Political Progress and Investment

The Mostar project was fundamentally political in nature. The development or reconstruction component was there as a tool to support political goals. This led in Mostar in 1994/95 (as also later in Sarajevo in 1996 and 1997) to a linkage between political progress and financial investment. A refusal by one party to implement some aspect of the Dayton Agreement led us to postpone some reconstruction projects.

At the beginning, I think we all felt this was reasonable and logical. Experience began to suggest otherwise and the position was largely abandoned. The idea was still being tried out elsewhere in Bosnia in 1997, and it did not appear to work then either.

Certainly, well directed investment may build up gratitude at the grass-roots level, and local political leaders may gain an advantage from cooperation so that they share those political benefits. Improving the conditions of life brings hope for the future, reduces grass-roots desperation, changes the political context, creates momentum and increases potential for progress. But there is a limit. The 'national interest', or the accumulation of the selfish interests of all persons of influence (which may be virtually the same thing), may be threatened. Then a threshold is passed and no amount of honest investment will cause an opponent to improve his political behaviour. Such attempts were perceived as bullying and were counter-productive.

I think that by 1996, we all realised that investment should be made regardless of political progress. The exception to this rule would be a project intended for a specific objective, the fulfilment of which was politically blocked. For example, housing for returning refugees would be wasted if one party prevented such a return. But in Mostar, most investment was of a broadly humanitarian or general developmental kind, such as housing, hospital or water supply projects, which, from the people's point of view, were necessary regardless of any political factors.

The Rades High Zone Water Project provided a salutary lesson. The Croat Mayor, Mr Brajković, persuaded Mr Koschnick to agree to a DM5 million project to create a water supply to a high zone which had never had a mains supply before. This was new work—not a repair project! This area (Cim, Ilići and Vihovići) was the hard-liners' heartland, and more than anything they wanted water. I suppose it was a political *quid pro quo*. A month later, Brajković created a serious riot, during which others made an attempt on Mr Koschnick's life. Some linkage!

Conclusion

Let me repeat my view that the EUAM was a seminal experiment. The 'Mostar model' allows the dynamic coordination and integration of different strands of policy; the sensitive shaping of tactics and strategy through intimate local knowledge and creative collaboration with local people and with other agencies on the ground; and lastly, very rapid (yet reliable) decision-making, so that the bureaucracy moves at least as fast as external events.

This model is based on decentralisation and delegation to an integrated task force at local level. The EC, in its Bosnia operation (except for Mostar) faces a self-inflicted problem, in that it has the wrong spatial pattern of decision-making authority. It is traditionally said that three variables define the correct pattern: participation potential; information-communication-decision costs; and overview advantage. What structure maximises the value of participation of people with important knowledge and skills (upon whom one relies for support)? What arrangement minimises the cost (including delay and misunderstanding) of information gathering and analysis, transmission, discussion and decision? What structure best captures the overview, that is, a wise understanding of the broad context?

In these respects, it seems clear that the centralisation in Brussels and low capability in theatre minimises participation potential and maximises communication costs. As regards overview advantage, the system could (in theory) perform well—but only if the centre defined strategy, responded rapidly to questions and exercised a monitoring/guidance role. As I described earlier, however, the centre has been, so far as Bosnian reconstruction is concerned, remote and unresponsive.

This is due, in my opinion, to two flaws. First, the Directorate-General concerned employs no technical experts in permanent positions, and displays a culture which misunderstands and marginalises the role of development professionals. I saw ample evidence of that. Also, and perhaps as a result, its administrative procedures are inappropriate for reconstruction work. That is the key reason why the EC (at the time of writing) has achieved little on the ground—except in Mostar. Only in Mostar were we free to create and continuously sharpen a practical system, which was hugely productive, *and* met with the approval of the Court of Auditors as well!

Chapter 4

Urban planning

Pre-war Mostar had a good planning system, and I found that local colleagues from all backgrounds understood its purpose and value. Judging from the number of people employed in the various institutes, it was overmanned and bureaucratic. But the results were visibly good. Sensible land-use zoning was properly enforced. There was virtually no illegal development before 1990, when institutional processes began to disintegrate in the run up to war. Roads and infrastructure were well coordinated with development, properly finished and maintained. Some oppressive architecture was created in the 1950s, but more recently most projects or buildings had stylish, individual designs, and there were fewer aesthetic crimes than in the average west European city. Public landscape was surprisingly lavish. Conservation of the historic patrimony was well done in terms of the overall urban scene and also of individual buildings, although the approach to the repair of the Old Town was too interventionist.

Urban planning before the 1960s was, in all our countries, largely a matter of physical design, and most planners were, in fact, architects. The scope then expanded to incorporate concerns for economic and social development. Also the approach to implementation, in terms of finance and organisation, became far more diverse and dynamic. The stress shifted from the plan to the action, and the scope expanded from design of layout and appearance to encompass the whole urban process.

Now, therefore, one sees 'planning' (so-called) as central to the whole business of urban life. In Mostar, this mechanism was shattered, and I believed strongly that the recovery of this system was a vital objective for the EUAM and particularly that it was a vehicle to build unification.

Structure Plan for All Mostar

In October 1994 I asked both sides to nominate a chief planner, to join with me in setting up an All-Mostar Strategic Planning Team. At that time, no one had any ideas about the future pattern of local government in Mostar, and the national government did not exist in a form acceptable to both sides. Indeed the war was still in progress a few miles north of the city. As a result, we had no central ministries to consult and could not place our system in the context of a national system. An *ad hoc* spirit prevailed.

I proposed a two-tier system, in which the two existing municipalities continued as (shall I say) 'borough' councils and a new entity, a 'city council', was set up as (essentially) a cooperative forum to handle whole-town strategic questions. I submitted a paper to Mr Koschnick, arguing that some such pragmatic approach would be accepted by both sides, whereas a single integrated council would not be accepted by the Croats. I saw the Joint Strategic Planning Team as the forerunner of such a city council.

Mr Koschnick did not respond positively since he envisaged at that time a conventional single-tier system. By early 1996, it became clear that this would not work, and a two-tier model was adopted as a basis for the 1996 elections. Since the mandate ended in July 1996, this left no time to build a functioning city administrative service.

Local experts were, thank goodness, very enthusiastic in principle about a joint structure plan. The team started work in spring 1995. The leader was my Croat co-head, Boro Puljić, and his deputy was Mrs Zijada Humo, a Muslim planner. They worked in EUAM offices, which was a safe neutral territory. Each side contributed five experts. The EUAM contributed three staff—my deputy, Francesco Aiello; Marica Raspudić, who is a talented urban designer; and Pero Marianović, the Professor of Computing at both Mostar and Zagreb Universities. I wrote a technical brief for the team, and all parties signed a contract.

The brief was conventional, covering demography, strategic land use, transportation, urban infrastructure, environment and economic development, with a stress on investment programming and finance. Work was very slow, as the experts struggled to reconcile the obvious conflicts. But they believed strongly in the mission and worked hard and sincerely. Work was halted by the riot of February 1996. This created a tremendous political convulsion, the ripples of which spread far and wide. I did not succeed in restarting the work before the end of the mandate.

However, a reasonably sound Report of Survey and Analysis was completed and presented. It was not possible to present a plan. I regard that as one of our more significant failures. Taking a positive view, however, we did prove that both sides had the will and capability to cooperate in a warm and constructive spirit. The Rome Conference and the resulting City Statute on which the 1996 elections were based, envisaged planning as the main function of the City Council. One must hope that this early experiment will form a solid foundation for that.

Local Plans

I envisaged local and action area plans as the task of lower-tier councils, with the caveat that a formal inter-tier cooperation mechanism be established, to permit the city council to direct the borough councils (Croat and Muslim) on strategic issues. I commissioned a Croatian consultant, Milan Karlovac, to prepare a local plan for the

Musala area, which is the heart of Austro-Hungarian East Mostar, including the Hotel Neretva, Austrian baths and music school. This was completed.

We also wished to prepare local plans for the Stari Grad or Old Town (the Ottoman core including the Old Bridge) and also for the adjacent Brankovac neighbourhood. I had already commissioned a British consultancy to work on urban infrastructure. I asked them to write technical briefs for these plans, which they did. The EUAM was unable to allocate the necessary funds, and the work did not proceed. I think there is a lesson here. The EU stressed investment in physical objects but was less concerned with repairing the process of urban management. We must hope that the EU reflects on the issue. The problem in Mostar was that after two-and-a-half years of EU involvement, the city had been massively repaired in a physical sense, but had really no sustainable financial or administrative mechanism. I had hoped that the plans (and the damage data-base, which is described below,) would provide a framework for managing repair. This did not happen, and so we proceeded in a pragmatic, *ad hoc* spirit.

The last local plan to be mentioned was for the 'Central Zone'. This is discussed in detail in the next section. This zone incorporates all the major public facilities of the city and is shared by both sides. My staff and myself drafted a plan for this area and completed it by July 1996. The intention was to provide a basis for international investment in a zone of huge political significance. It remains to be seen if any use is made of it. The Italian Government was EU President at the time, and the then Foreign Minister, Susanna Agnelli, made a serious public commitment to develop the plan using Italian funds.

A Diplomatic Interlude

The efforts to create a single unified city council (as the MOU required) led to protracted negotiations in late 1995. As described above, I had proposed a two-tier system of government—one Croat and one Muslim council, cooperating on strategic matters via a city council (to the extent which mutual pragmatic interests required). Mr Koschnick came to the same view, but the Dayton Agreement envisaged three lower-tier municipalities on each side—a total of six. He also wanted a central zone, which would belong to neither side—or rather to both. He mentioned the District of Columbia and Canberra as models. This central zone would break the confrontation line in those parts of the city where it did not follow the River Neretva. In my opinion, this was an excellent idea.

A long series of meetings were held with both sides to agree the boundaries of the central zone. The Croats made emotional speeches about who had died on which street and how it must forever be part of their homeland: clearly they wanted a tiny zone—if any at all. The Muslims naturally wanted a very big zone. They had all the logical arguments: but, as Sir Martin Garrod—a former military man—sagely pointed out, no side victorious in war will quickly surrender its gains. That is reality.

Sadly, no progress was made by our diplomats. My personal impression was that they became bogged down because they had not found a technical framework to structure the debate. I then suggested that urban planners could perhaps create clarity by applying some objective methodology. Mr Koschnick and Sir Martin generously agreed to hear our ideas.

We proposed the following criteria. The central zone should include all joint public facilities, such as the main post office, railway station, main bus station, joint police headquarters, grammar school, public utility offices, the Hotel Ero (seat of the European Union) etc. It should exclude housing areas, but should include enough vacant or destroyed land to provide for the four Federal Ministries which the Dayton Agreement required to be located in Mostar. The area and its facilities should be accessible from federal highways without the need to enter via the local territory of either side. The boundary should be as small and tight as possible (subject to these requirements) and be divided equally in area between both sides. I suggested that these criteria be negotiated before lines were drawn on paper, but that the boundary then be devised in a purely logical way.

This approach was accepted, and my colleagues and I prepared a proposal, including calculations and a map. With the agreement of Administrator Koschnick, Sir Martin and I presented this to both sides. The Muslim side was led by Prime Minister Silajdić and the Catholic side by the Croatian Defence Minister Šušak. To everyone's amazement, the Croat side (under some duress from Zagreb) immediately agreed. The Muslim side did not, although in my view it was the best feasible deal from their point of view.

Mr Koschnick then proposed that he arbitrate. He did so three days later and issued a decree which defined a large central zone incorporating a housing area penetrating far into Croat territory. This satisfied the Muslim politicians but outraged the Croats. The Croat Major, Mijo Brajković, then called over local radio for a popular demonstration against Mr Koschnick to be held outside the Hotel Ero. This took place within a few minutes. It was joined by extremists, who tried to sack the Hotel Ero and, more seriously, surrounded and attacked Mr Koschnick's car as he was leaving. His car was armoured and, showing impressive courage he survived with no loss of cheerfulness and calm.

At that time the Italian Ambassador and the Director-General of the Italian Foreign Ministry were resident in Mostar. Ambassador Mattacotta supported the town planners' proposal (having discussed it with my planning colleague, Francesco Aiello) and reported this to their Minister, Mrs Agnelli. Shortly afterwards, the so-called Rome Conference was held. On that occasion, the Muslim side agreed with the proposed boundary. The Rome Conference had, in effect, overturned Mr Koschnik's arbitration decision, and he resigned.

The agreement opened the way to the Mostar elections, which were most efficient and produced an elected city council and a new mayor of all Mostar. This fulfilled the requirement of the Dayton Agreement and allowed the European Union to hand over its power to an elected local authority. Whether that authority will, in due course, find a way to function effectively on behalf of all the citizens is another question. For me it was a most interesting experience. Does it perhaps show how the naive logic of sensitive, neutral experts can open a way forward on such problems which politicians and diplomats might not discover unaided?

Data Management

From the beginning, I had an aim of producing a data-base and an information management system. There were several purposes to this. First, we needed to manage the investment in building repair—to know what the damage was, how to direct investment, and where it had already been directed as time went by. Second, we needed to relate this to the beneficiaries, and that would require a link to the property ownership record and to data on current population characteristics, such as ethnicity and overcrowding. Displacement of population on a huge scale meant that property rights were usually not held by the current occupier. The EUAM wanted to facilitate the return of refugees and displaced persons to their homes, this aim deriving from the MOU and subsequently the Dayton Agreement. One could foresee that the investment in repair would be in part conditioned by that objective.

Moreover, if some element of investment were to come from the owner, and if EUAM investment were to be repaid in the long term by absentee owners as a condition of their return, then a good data-base would be needed to control the countless thousands of cases which would arise Such repayment, however slow, would recycle finance and permit the successor of the EUAM to carry on investing.

The third reason concerned infrastructure. The records had been imperfect before the war and in any case were partly lost or destroyed. Efficient management of the water system from an engineering standpoint, for example, required up-to-date records. Also, the efficient collection of charges, and the administration of subsidies to consumers, was vitally important if we were to lay the basis for a financially sustainable system. We provided large numbers of meters and appropriate hardware and software. But in addition a sound data-base was necessary.

Finally, of course, all this could also provide valuable inputs to the work of the urban planners. We made considerable strides forward, and the remainder of this chapter describes some of the main initiatives.

Base Mapping

The Spanish and Belgian Army Geographical Institutes both tendered to supply digitised maps of Mostar by aerial survey and ground checking at 1–5000 and 1–10 000 scales, with related computer equipment and training of local officials. The contract was awarded to the Spanish, who were the lowest tenderers. It proved impossible, in the event, to fly the area at the right time of the year, due to security factors: the Serbs were still shelling the city occasionally and UNPROFOR would not authorise flights. This caused a delay. Enquiries revealed that the British Army had recent stereographic pairs of the whole area, and they kindly agreed to allow the Spanish Army to use them.

When the maps and software were delivered in September 1995, a training course was held for local experts in the technical training centre which my department had established previously.

Building Damage Data-base

Faced with the enormous scale of damage, and the challenge of managing the investment process, I decided to commission a survey of damage and a computerised data-base covering the zone of serious damage. This would record the location, size, use, damage, and investment details as they arose. I planned on linking this later to a property rights database and also the infrastructure cadastre. At the outset, however, I proposed that repair investment be entered as it occurred. Subsequent claims or proposals could be checked, so that we could prevent irrationality, false prioritisation, duplication, corruption etc.

I did not go out to tender, since I had not the capacity in September 1994 to manage that, nor indeed could we afford the delay. I went directly to the only agency with the capability for such work already in theatre, namely the Gesellschaft für Technische Zusammenarbeit (GTZ), a German Government Agency. I prepared a brief and received their written proposal in January 1995. The contract was signed, and the work completed by March. The survey system envisaged six categories of damage. Standard repair cost rates allowed computation of financial budget requirements by building type and location. A large team of local surveyors was employed by GTZ, and their work took ten weeks. Coloured survey maps of use, damage and cost and tabulation of statistics were delivered, as well as the data-base files on disk and an operating manual. The team was directed in Mostar by Kuno von Falkenstein, a German architect. I had asked the EU to support the establishment of a small team to operate the system but this was not forthcoming, and so the survey material and the management system were not fully utilised.

Population Census

The last census had occurred shortly before the start of the first war. Since then, of course, ethnic cleansing and internal displacement had made that census meaningless. We did not have time to conduct a full census, but needed to know urgently basic facts on ethnic composition by area, and the degree of overcrowding or underoccupation. A sample census of a fairly simple kind was proposed.

The Swedish Government census office was chosen by the Refugee Adviser, Bo

Kaelfors. Their team was led by a census expert, who was also an architect, Ingmar Saevfors. I asked Saevfors and the GTZ team to cooperate together, so that the software and files on buildings and people could be conveniently linked. The census was completed by March 1995.

It contained some political bombshells. The two local parties had argued that their population was larger than it truly was, in order, perhaps, to claim more humanitarian aid, amongst other reasons. The ethnic composition was also used as a basis for political argument. The document became hot property, and the Diplomatic Adviser embargoed its circulation, preferring to keep it under lock and key.

The Cadastral Institutes

The Cadastral Institute had split into two independent parts—east and west—as a result of the war. All informatic, survey and office equipment was destroyed (or stolen). The records themselves were intact, but were entirely held by the Croat side. For political reasons, in 1994 they refused to allow access by the Muslim side (and, of course, by the EUAM as well). In an emergency situation, this obviously did not matter. But our task was to restore normal life, and a survey and property rights record is an extremely important part of the normal functioning of all modern cities.

Therefore, in mid-1995, I proposed to both institutes that the EUAM replace all their equipment and vehicles, provided that they agreed to unify into a single entity. The two directors said they and their staff were eager to agree, but that this was a political matter. The Croat politicians would not agree. Negotiations proceeded for six months. Quickly, as a gesture of good will, the Croat side agreed to supply copies of any records which the Muslims or the EUAM asked for. This they did efficiently, but they would not part with the records themselves.

In the end, I recommended that the EUAM should compromise. We therefore purchased equipment to the value of DM 250 000, split equally between the two sides. They both agreed to update the infrastructure cadastre and resurvey certain key parts of the city (at no charge to us) and they also agreed to share all information between them. This was a significant step forwards. They had already proved willing to work together, and I wanted to reward and strengthen a movement in the right direction.

The equipment was procured by us and handed over at a small ceremony in May 1996. I drafted a deed of gift by which the beneficiaries held the items in trust subject to several requirements. For instance, the items should be maintained in accordance with the manufacturers' instructions; they should not be disposed of; they should not be used to support warlike purposes; the documents and data produced should be available to the public with no restriction and at reasonable cost; and so on.

Conclusion

Clearly, the urban planning work was not a great success if one measures it in terms of 'deliverables' actually delivered—whether one looks at documents or at institutions and processes created and made to function efficiently. My personal view is that success in these terms could and should have been attained. Perhaps I am too much an optimist. But it could be said that the entire Mostar project was one vast optimistic experiment; one would not need to be very cynical to see it as 'a triumph of hope over experience'. I base my unapologetic optimism on the fact that the locals on both sides believed in planning—apparently quite strongly, and they proved that in action. After 18 months (or less) the EU had gone through a considerable learning curve in Mostar and discovered that once the humanitarian emergency is past, the task of repairing the institutions and processes of urban management is, if anything, even more basic than the repair of damaged physical objects.

To make a positive interpretation, it is fair to say that we proved that both sides wanted to cooperate in strategic planning and control of a unified city, and—more to the point—that they were actually able to take the early steps. That is a demonstration. Also it is a foundation upon which the new city council can build its primary function, which emerged from the Dayton and Rome agreements, of urban planning.

Chapter 5

Project Management

This chapter aims to summarise the system for the implementation of construction projects, such as repair of public buildings, heavily damaged houses, water and sewerage infrastructure etc. The repair of lightly damaged houses—in which thousands of properties received minor repairs—was handled differently, and that is described later.

I was pressed by Mr Koschnick to start action as soon as I arrived in Mostar, and so a system had to be created out of the blue immediately. I devised it, and wrote the contract forms in a few hours. With no time for reflection and consultation, I had to rely on familiar principles, in the full knowledge that I might be making errors. Happily, and more by luck than judgement, the system created during my first week proved to be durable and successful, although details were refined as time went by.

I did the (to me) obvious thing. I envisaged the appointment of local independent consultants to prepare detailed contract documents (including drawings and bills of quantity) and to supervise on site. I wrote a consultancy contract for the purpose and fixed a fairly generous fee. Construction work would go to competitive tender, and I wrote a construction contract based loosely on normal British forms, but greatly simplified.

Contractors should be pre-qualified, so that a tender committee could normally simply choose the cheapest offer. I would appoint, as soon as possible, project managers to run this process. Contract documents would be as full as possible so as to minimise arguments and claims later. Variations, extensions of time and payments should be authorised by issue of a standard form and approved by the signatures of consultant, the EUAM project manager and me. I felt that one manager could handle contracts to the value of about DM5 million per year. At local cost rates, this was about a two per cent fee equivalent (if secretaries, cars and office costs were added). In the event, appointment of staff was so restricted by the EU that the fee at peak activity was one per cent. At one stage, a particular individual was running projects at the rate of equivalent to DM19 million per year!

The approach seemed to me normal and obvious. Certainly I could claim no credit for wisdom or prescience. Some time later, however, I began to realise that it was controversial. It differed from the approach of the World Bank, which did not become involved in implementation management at all. The EC had never before set up such project management teams at site level, with delegated powers to write, sign and supervise contracts. Local municipalities wanted us to give them the money to administer. They objected to our 'hands-on' approach. They expected the EUAM to be a provider of money and no more than that. Many non-governmental organisations wanted us to give them our finance, on the basis of a package deal in which they would prepare designs, procure materials, employ labour and, in effect, act as 'cost-plus' contractor. Finally, some builders wanted to act as design/build contractors, tendering on outline plans and a lump sum price. There are many different ways to implement projects, and choosing the right way is the most significant decision of all.

The Roles of Client and Beneficiary

One key question was role definition. In particular, I had to define the contractual position of the EUAM, and this decision had to be taken immediately. I decided to regard the EUAM as the client of the contractors, and to regard the building owner as a beneficiary. Since the EUAM was paying, I assumed we should direct and control projects—with the beneficiaries' consent. Owners signed both consultancy and construction contracts. They checked and approved contract documents and signed technical acceptance protocols upon completion. Beyond that, their role was to provide access to the site for the contractor and others.

The municipalities wanted to take the project implementation role, and—more or less—this is what the World Bank agreed to when it arrived in Bosnia eighteen months later. They instigated a Project Implementation Unit based in the Ministry of Finance in Sarajevo. They made credits available to the government, which then signed contracts and executed projects. The Bank signed no contracts and had no supervisory role. This model is rational from many points of view and has been successful. But the EUAM was in a different position. It was itself, *de jure*, the actual authority in the city, whereas the Bank is, of course, a banker to government. Without detracting from the overall success of the Bosnian activity of the Bank, it is fair to argue that their approach has a few side-effects. For example, some of the government elite had bought into the contracting industry. They were also, of course, directing the activity of the Civil Service, which was managing the expenditure of the money provided by the Bank.

The Role of the Consultant

On each project, an independent local consultancy firm was hired to prepare a full and detailed set of drawings and bills of quantities, upon which shortlisted contractors then tendered. The same consultant provided site supervision services. I wrote a 'Standard Form of Consultancy Contract' for the purpose. Consultants were generally chosen for the quality of their work, and in particular, their ability to complete accurate and detailed documents—the aim being to minimise the need for variations and extra costs later. We fixed a generous fee of three per cent for design and two per cent for supervision, based on the cost of the works. We did not tender on fees; we chose to reward consultants properly and then demand that they did a thoroughly professional job. In Former Yugoslavia, independent and self-regulating professions (in the western sense) did not exist. Design firms were either municipal or state departments, or else they were divisions of state construction or investment companies. The professional man or woman had relatively little sense of personal responsibility. If, therefore, an error or omission led to extra cost, the designer was not punished. The state paid the price. I believe that I was the first person to sack an architect in Bosnia since the Second World War for producing poor documents and failing to respect cost limits. My local staff saw very clearly the value of independent consultancy. Hasan Ćemalović, for instance, was acting President of the Bosnian Society of Architects. He wished to transform it on western lines, and asked the Royal Institute of British Architects for advice. It was a proud moment for him when, in 1996, the International Union of Architects (UIA) admitted the Bosnian Society to membership.

The consultant was given a 'Scope of Works' document, written by the EU Project Manager, which summarised the range and quality of required works. An indicative budget was also given, derived from a simple cost data-base which my local staff and THW (Technisches Hilfswerk, the German federal emergency organisation) had created.

Consultants were pressed by us to work too quickly. We were given a very tight timescale by the EU, and our lack of realism caused documents to be more superficial and incomplete than I would have wished. But even so, I tried to resist unrealistic timescales. It is better to prepare a careful design at the beginning, since it saves time, cost and confusion later. In Bosnia there was no system of professional indemnity insurance. Consultants made some culpable errors, but it was unrealistic to sue them for this. Also, of course, there were no functioning courts. We could have refused to pay their fees, and I used this as a threat on occasions.

Registration of Contractors

At the beginning, we drew up a list of pre-qualified contractors who had applied for registration. We inspected each one to check their equipment, premises, manpower etc. We obtained a list of previous work. Each contractor was required to complete a form giving this information. They were categorised by size and type of work. In reality, of course, many firms had lost much (or all) of their assets in the war, and many of their key personnel were scattered around the country. We could not refuse to give work to such firms, since that would penalise them twice and would also conflict with the aim of recovery.

To some extent, the Equipment Hire Service and Small Enterprise Grant Programme helped builders to re-equip themselves. But I believe that the payment of large advances (such as 40 per cent upon signature of contract and receipt of a guarantee), and also the generally rapid transfer of money, had a tremendously beneficial effect on the cash flow of builders, and that this was the main factor enabling them to perform so well. The criteria for the registration of contractors were liberally applied. The main advantage was that dishonest firms were eliminated. We also pre-qualified firms from other towns and cities. The Mostar contractors did not like this, since it increased competition. But it had a tremendously beneficial effect on them.

Preparation of Tender Shortlists

We generally shortlisted five or six firms for each tender. I proposed the firms after discussion with my project managers and local counterparts. We kept a register chart of such invitations, so that it was clear to everyone that all registered firms had been given roughly equal chances. Firms performing badly, or failing to cooperate, knew that their chances of tendering would be reduced (or ultimately, they would be crossed off the register altogether). A logical and demonstrably fair approach to this matter was vitally important in Mostar. Big money was at stake, and a lot of pressure was put on me (through several channels) to include certain firms or exclude others. Much of this pressure came at the political level, and the slightest smell of unfairness or inconsistency, let alone corruption, would have had consequences beyond the merely commercial plane. I had to have a completely fair and correct reply to each accusation. In the end, people realised that we were playing a straight bat, and a degree of trust and respect arose.

Firms were invited by the EU to tender by means of standard letter. We required each firm to accept or refuse in writing. The firms then collected the drawings and bill of quantities from our office, and generally we gave them two or three weeks to submit a priced bill. The bid was submitted on a standard form. The time for tendering was too short, but we were in a hurry. Builders made occasional errors in consequence, which sometimes led them into financial problems. If disputes arose I always stuck closely to the letter of the contract. But if there was room for interpretation, I erred on the side of generosity to the builder. This allowed a good atmosphere to develop and got the jobs finished smoothly.

Tender Selection

I proposed a tendering committee and drafted some rules of operation. Each tender had to be submitted in a sealed envelope, of course. The cheapest tender was chosen, on the basis that tender documents (i.e. drawings and bills of quantities) were complete and accurate, and that all tenderers were registered and therefore deemed to be competent. I met a lot of resistance to this idea. I was pressed to evaluate bids on the quality of the firm as well as price. The Yugoslav tradition was like this. But in reality it would have been impossible to make an incontestable decision if a committee had to trade off incommensurable factors. This became very clear at the outset. Local politicians tried to pressure the tender committee (and in particular, myself) to award jobs to their preferred companies, on the grounds that they were the 'best'. The door was then open for endless delay and debate, as well as corruption and non-transparency. Most surprising to me was the preference of some EU colleagues for such multi-factorial evaluation. I had to dig in my heels.

The two sides were politically represented on the committee, and tenderers were also invited. There was a quorum of three EU officers plus the chairman. The local representatives could speak but not vote. The committee met every week. After the tenders were opened and recorded, my staff prepared a written analysis. This was considered one week later, and the committee made a formal award. This procedure was very effective. Strong argument rarely arose and decisions were quick, clean and transparent. Often five or six major contracts were awarded each week and the committee meetings rarely lasted for more than an hour.

Contract Preparation and Signature

I drafted a relatively simple Standard Form of Building Contract. It envisaged a large advance payment, monthly stage (or interim) payments, and a final payment upon practical completion. A 'retention fund' of 10 per cent was held for the 'defects liability period'. This was paid to the builder when any defects in his work had been corrected. When the banking system recovered in mid-1995, a bank guarantee was required to cover the advance payment. After signature of the contract, this guarantee took a week or two to obtain. The advance payment was then made by bank transfer.

Financial Control

At the beginning there was no local banking system. Also the EUAM had no finance department. I simply wrote a standard letter to the Head of Internal Administration, who took banknotes from the safe and drove in an armoured car to the builder's office. This was the 'wild west' phase. There was no official budget, so I prepared my own which, *faute de mieux*, was accepted by the Administrator. A little later the EC sent out a Finance Director. The finance system became functional about six months after the beginning of the process. It worked from then until July 1996 very effectively. Decisions were made and money transferred at lighting speed. Contractors and beneficiaries were very appreciative and responded by working cooperatively and quickly. The Court of Auditors reported this in a very positive way.

Every major investment decision required approval on political grounds by the Administrator. A form was devised for this. This form was submitted by the investing department. It was signed also by the Finance Director in order to check that the credits were actually available. All contracts similarly required his visa. When a payment was requested, two forms—one page each—were completed. The first form was referred to as 'payment request'. The second form recorded all payments made on the contract, such as advance, stage and final payments. By this means, we could check and control the overall position on each contract at each stage. The EU financial regulations provided the framework. The Authorising Officer, the Accounting Officer, the Financial Controller and the Superior Authority have ascribed roles within these regulations. I acted as an Authorising Officer, defining the project and submitting the request for payment. The Accounting Officer maintained correct records. The Financial Controller gave authority for payment after ascertaining that the credits were available, the names and account numbers were correct and so on. If he refused to agree, then the matter was to be decided by the Superior Authority. The EC had delegated this role to the Mostar Administrator. This act of delegation was immensely important, since it allowed decision-making to be rapid and well informed. But, in fact, not one dispute arose between me and the Financial Controller. He sometimes asked for more information so that a full written justification was provided to his satisfaction. This could introduce a delay of a day in the approval process. Nonetheless, it was normal to secure approval within two days and the bank transfer might then take a week. In my view, this extraordinarily efficient finance machine was the secret of our success. Great credit for this must go to the Finance Director, Klaus von Helldorff, and his excellent deputy, Frank Marshall.

The only problem arose from occasional delays in the staged release of financial tranches by Brussels. But the visit of the Court of Auditors solved this problem. They clearly saw that Brussels' attempt at control was counter-productive, and recommended that all Mostar funds be released at one fell swoop. This was agreed and from then onwards, all such problems were solved.

Variation Orders and Extensions of Time

The contract envisaged 'variation orders' and 'extensions of time'. This is a normal provision, but a few administrative colleagues found the idea hard to accept. In a ruined building, it is impossible to see accurately the condition before works start. Even a first-class architect, working on a reasonable timescale, will be unable to specify and measure with complete accuracy. But in Bosnia, we had a profession which was massively depleted by ethnic cleansing. Before the war, they were accustomed to prepare inaccurate documents on the basis that the builder would do what was needed and the communist state would pay the extra cost. I stressed the need for precision, but one cannot change attitudes overnight, nor would it be fair to expect that. But, in any case, we pressed consultants to work faster than normal or proper. We budgeted for a 10 per cent contingency sum—a low figure—and it was quite unusual for this to be exceeded. The contract made clear that the builder was to check the site and contract documents in detail. If an item were omitted in the bill of quantities, but implied by the description—in other words, if an item was clearly necessary in order to accomplish the described work—then it would not be paid as an extra. In approving variation orders, I tried to be very fair and even sympathetic to the builder. I took the view that in Mostar it would be counter-productive to press the builders too hard. The result of that would have been delay and bad quality. Indeed, it could lead to jobs being abandoned. The lack of a legal system would have made it impossible to sue builders through the courts. The absence of an enforcement mechanism altered my tactical perspective.

But suppose that we had forced firms into bankruptcy: this would have conflicted with the EU aim of strengthening the commercial sector. Indeed, in pursuit of this aim, the Economic Department gave a lot of grant money to companies. On the other hand, of course, one must be strict enough to develop a sense of discipline and responsibility. I believe we struck the correct balance. As a result, the builders respected us for our rigour and our fairness. Jobs were completed with no serious delays and to a reasonable quality. I think most builders behaved well. The out-turn costs were, without exception, relatively low. I remember a visit in November 1996 by World Bank staff, when costs were discussed. Our building costs were generally two-thirds of their costs. I attribute this to strict competition and a 'hands-on' management system.

Completion and Defects Liability

When the contractor served notice, an inspection was held and a Technical Acceptance Report was issued, signed by the Beneficiary, the Municipal Building Inspector and the Project Manager. The keys were handed over to the Beneficiary and the building was occupied. Before the expiry of the bank guarantee, another inspection was held to detect any defects which were clearly attributable to the builder or designer.

The contract proposed a defects liability period of one year. A retention fund of 10 per cent was to be held and paid to the builder when an inspection was done and defects corrected. This is normal, of course. But after a year or so, the EC objected to this, because it wished all obligations, whether legal or financial, to end at the completion of the mandate, on 23 July 1996. I had not understood this point, and perhaps the EC had not considered the practical implications either. We therefore decided to pay the last 10 per cent if the builder could present a bank guarantee for the same sum for the liability period. This would be assigned to the local beneficiary, upon our departure, so that he could obtain redress for defects if necessary. Later, the work of the EU was extended from July 1996 to April 1997. At that point, the EC objected to the procedure (which had been instigated at their earlier request!). We were no longer permitted to pay retention money in exchange for a guarantee.

This caused a lot of unpleasant argument with builders, who had grown accustomed to the previous situation. It created some cash-flow problems for builders. This state of affairs lasted from August 1996 to January 1997. Then the EC faced the urgent need to terminate its operation in Mostar, and we reverted to the previous system of guarantees. But, shortly afterwards, the position changed back. The moral of this story is that clarity and consistency is vital, and this is best assured by leaving construction professionals in charge of construction.

Alternative Models

There were at least two other project implementation 'models' used in Mostar, which, in my opinion, did not work so well. On some new-build health projects, we tendered on design and construction together. With five or six firms tendering, the designs submitted were only sketches and the prices were lump sums without priced complete bills of quantity. We were generally obliged to choose an acceptable design at a higher price. The absence of a priced bill made further negotiation difficult. The contractors were inventing details during the works, but they lacked the experience and sophistication to undertake 'fast-track' procedures. For us, it was not easy to control the job. The Head of Health Department, an excellent medical doctor, overruled my advice on this point. He was pressed by contractors to do so, because it was the customary practice in former Yugoslavia. They did not like to be controlled by detailed documents and independent professionals. After he left, I felt obliged on one large job to require the successful tenderer to prepare a full design and a full bill of quantities before construction started. This took more time at the start, but it led to better quality and value. I also suspect that increased clarity saved time and trouble overall.

The second model was typically followed by foreign non-governmental organisations (NGOs) in Bosnia. In one case in Mostar, it failed. In mid-1994 the NGO signed a package-deal contract with the EUAM to repair blocks of damaged apartments. There was no form of competition. Then the NGO appointed an expatriate Project Manager, who hired a consultant to prepare plans. He selected by a loose tendering process a labour-only contractor, and himself procured materials, stored them and delivered them to site. All management on site was then undertaken by the Project Manager. However, a good local contractor is better able to procure local materials than a small foreign NGO. Also, of course, he can be held responsible for coordinating labour and materials. The NGO was free to ignore the consultant's drawings, which it did. The EUAM had not hired the consultant, and the NGO refused to let us see the plans. We had no control at all. Because this was not (for the EUAM) a commercial contract awarded after price competition, we had to insist that we inspect all the NGO's accounts prior to the final settlement. But they could not present proper accounts. Furthermore, the repaired buildings leaked quite a lot because the design was ignored and construction was incomplete and poorly executed. The NGO was a charity and had no resources, so it could not be sued.

Some NGOs are excellent, but not all. In any case, I could not see the advantage of such an arrangement in principle, even if the NGO were excellent. Things went most smoothly when we ourselves had direct contracts with an independent consultant and a contractor; when the design and bills were properly checked by us; when a commercially-motivated builder organised both labour and materials; and when our consultant 'policed' the builder.

The Role of Local EU Project Managers

I had, at the peak, eight managers on construction projects. Their task included briefing consultants; checking their drawings and bills of quantities; proposing tender shortlists; analysing tenders after opening; inspecting works on site; checking progress and sorting out problems; checking invoices (after the consultant had done so); and preparing payment requests. At the start, I asked for several expatriates, but member states did not respond very well and in the end I relied mainly on local experts. They were from Mostar, Sarajevo or, in one case, Zagreb. I chose them with care. Several were very senior in their profession. I was careful to praise them and support them practically and psychologically. Quite soon, they became proud to work for the EUAM and believed strongly in our common mission. Only by delegation to trusted and highly motivated staff could we have accomplished so much in so short a period. Of course, they were operating in the framework of a clear system of project administration. There was a simple, clear and practical routine. My trust in my local staff earned me some regard from other local people, and I avoided the charge of 'neo-colonialism' which many organisations in Bosnia suffered from. I think that, in a relatively advanced country like Bosnia, it is better to rely on local staff, provided you earn their respect and loyalty, than to import a large number of expatriates—unless, of course, some special expertise (not otherwise available) is needed. They speak the language and know the local system. They can resolve difficulties which no expatriate could.

I said many times that, as it turned out, the reconstruction work was a local effort, for which local people should take the credit. Europe provided the money, the system and the leadership, but the real work to rebuild Mostar was not done by foreigners. This is an important message, since people only respect and value the results of their own work. It is a matter of pride.

Ownership and Use of Investments

Problems arose in a few cases when the owner of a building was different from the intended operator. The property registration records (cadastre and 'Grundbuch') for the whole city were held by the west side, and they refused access for the first year. We had some—mercifully few—cases where the owner seized a building which we repaired for another intended occupier. For example, we repaired and equipped a 'training centre' which was seized by another party who claimed ownership. We repaired an archive building for cultural purposes, which the east municipality later leased to the Iranian Consulate. We repaired a youth centre, which was taken over by a radio station. The point is that, first, we should have checked ownership records, and second, prepared legal agreements as to subsequent use. I got my fingers burnt twice, and after that was more careful. The important thing is to prepare full and proper legal documents covering ownership and utilisation before investment is committed.

Conclusion

Several people told me that the system described here had revolutionised the attitude of many contractors and consultants in Bosnia. It created a commercial mentality and a sharpened awareness of personal responsibility. The system could only work, however, on the basis of delegation from Brussels of financial authority and professional freedom. Rapid decisions and rapid payment were the key to success. Where normal EC procedure was applied, little has been achieved.

I also think that the World Bank's 'hands-off' procedure drives up costs. The role of NGOs as management contractors, and also the use of 'design-build' contracts, were of dubious merit in the Mostar situation. It was hard to control and led to more work and expense than it saved.

Chapter 6

Housing

Without doubt, the greatest single effort in the reconstruction of Mostar was housing repair. It transformed the overall aspect of the city. The view from the by-pass road, which was routed over the eastern hillsides, revealed a scene of utter devastation in 1994. Most roofs were destroyed and the mess of ruination was visible everywhere. Two years later, the same viewpoint revealed a sea of freshly tiled roofs, and pristine white apartment houses. The scale of the change was remarkable. Well over 6000 dwellings were repaired at a cost of DM40 million. It is, however, far easier to spend money on a few high-value buildings than to spend the same money on hundreds of low-value buildings, since each such building has a separate site, a separate owner, separate documentation and so on. The administrative complexity is formidable, and also, of course, housing generates more passion than other building types, since it affects each family more intimately. The scope for anger and resentment was there on a large scale, but, in spite of terrific pressures (particularly on municipal officials and THW [Technisches Hilfswerk]) we sustained our effort and the success was acknowledged at grass-roots level.

The local municipalities had already begun to survey damage in mid-1994. But they had no computing resources, and data were gathered in an unstructured way, so that it was hard to deduce priorities, allocate resources, manage action and monitor change. The EUAM made its own survey, which is described in Chapter 4. It became clear to me, however, that the choice of individual beneficiaries could only be done by the municipalities. At first, this opened the way to manipulation by the rich for selfish motives, and by the powerful for party advantage. But a relatively tiny EU staff had neither the time nor the detailed knowledge to carry out this task. In Chapter 7, Andreas Seebacher of THW suggests that the EU should have made a greater effort in this direction. The issue is clearly a controversial one.

The damage data-base categorised dwellings into light, medium and heavy damage; that is, less than 30 per cent, less than 50 per cent and less than 70 per cent damage. More than 70 per cent damage was regarded as a write-off.

Light Damage Housing Repair

In September 1994, as soon as I arrived, Mr Koschnick insisted on immediate action, although we had no data on damage or need. However, local colleagues had a lot of constructive suggestions, and we decided to launch into a massive programme for repair of lightly damaged houses to be completed by Christmas, before the bad weather set in. There were obviously thousands of relatively sound houses rendered less than habitable due to holes in the roof and walls. To repair these would be relatively cheap and fast, but very cost-effective.

I sought as large a housing budget as I could, and DM10 million was accepted by Mr Koschnick. I immediately set up a housing committee. At the first meeting, I asked my local colleagues what was their best guess at an average cost per house for materials, and how many houses would need labour to be provided—or, in other words, how far was self-help feasible. A consensus emerged, and this was adopted— DM1500 per house for materials plus DM500 for labour on 50 per cent of the houses. The basis for this decision was crude, but we needed to act immediately. Given the budget, we proposed a programme of 3500 houses.

We restricted the maximum value per house, although efforts were made to circumvent this by a few people, who threatened municipal officials (Andreas Seebacher mentions this in Chapter 7). Only the external fabric could be repaired for this money. On later contracts, as we gained more experience and gathered more data, we extended the eligible scope of works to include water supply, toilets and electrical works. The cost limit was increased to DM3000 per house, and labour was made more freely available.

In 1994, I had to use what people and institutions were immediately available and fit for work. Technisches Hilfswerk had a rudimentary materials procurement and delivery capability, although it rapidly expanded in scale and gained great managerial competence by mid-1995. However, THW would work only in east Mostar, and in the west we employed the only available firm (Slavonija Trgovina) to procure and deliver materials. They did a good job, although it was on a smaller scale than that undertaken by THW. The local 'War Damage Commissions' had already assembled a team of (largely unqualified) surveyors. The municipal technical departments had a few staff, though the east side had no offices or equipment. Finally, there were a few contractors with some capability left: we chose Zidar in the east and Konstruktor in the west. Damage surveys and measurement of materials and labour would be done by the War Damage Commissions. The contractors would hire labour and manage it, whilst THW and Slavonija Trgovina would procure and deliver the material. The coordination of all these agencies would be done by the municipal technical agencies. On this basis, I wrote a contract specifically for repair of light damage.

But did the locals have the capacity? Not only were they without experienced staff, offices and equipment, they were also in a state of shock and despair. I therefore proposed to repair their destroyed office and to purchase equipment. This was acted on immediately. I also asked a Spanish NGO, Ingenieros Sin Fronteras, to devise the software for a project management system. They did this in continuous discussion with the local engineers and it proved to be invaluable in controlling the many thousands of separate operations. It also allowed us to prove that every Deutschmark could be accounted for, and it exposed cases of fraud early on and permitted us to stamp them out.

We also decided to pay for professional and manual work. This was controversial. We fixed the hourly rate for building workers. The notional times allowed for units of different operations were taken from the old Yugoslav *Book of Building Norms*. The labour contractor was paid a management fee. We also paid a small professional fee for survey and management. This was criticised. But, in the end, I believe I was right. It restored self-respect and enthusiasm, but also attracted skilled people from other less damaged towns, so that after six or nine months, we had fully-functioning professional and construction firms as well as a vigorous municipality. At the beginning, part of the salaries in the east was diverted to pay the soldiers and I was (correctly) accused of subsidising the Muslim war effort. Soon the war subsided, however, and we successfully insisted that workers should sign for the receipt of wages. This was abused for a short time, but private inquiries revealed that by mid-1995 all workers were receiving their correct pay. This approach helped to restore some normality to life.

We completed the first light damage repair by May 1995, though our target had been December 1994. Given the destruction of technical capacity and my own lack of staff (until January 1995) it was clear at the outset that a miracle would be needed to complete the repair of 3500 houses in three months. Later contracts of the same type in 1995/96 were completed on time. This was due not only to objective improvements in the construction sector, but also to the defeat of despair and hopelessness. Appendix One contains data on light damage repair contracts. Several other light damage programmes followed in 1995/96, but by early 1995 we felt able to contemplate the repair of more seriously damaged houses.

Medium and Heavy Damage Housing Repair Programme

The Refugee Adviser, Ambassador Bo Kaelfors, had the brief to facilitate the return of refugees and displaced persons. To repair houses which were already occupied was a humanitarian act, but did not create additional capacity. We therefore decided to tackle empty dwellings too. They were uninhabitable (or largely so) because heavily damaged.

Much of this housing was in the quasi-rural fringe of Mostar and we proposed to return farmers to these houses. This would also create a livelihood and boost food supply for the city. But there were also many such houses in the city proper. In many cases, we proposed to decant the population into their own houses thereby releasing space for others. In other cases, the houses had been owned by Serbs who clearly would not return for quite a long time. But nonetheless there was a serious question of legal principle and practice.

We therefore proposed a decree to the Administrator, which would give him powers to repair the dwellings of absent persons, and to allow others to occupy them, albeit subject to certain conditions. If the original owners returned, they had the power to reclaim the dwelling after giving notice, subject to their agreement to repay gradually to the public authorities the cost of repair. Mr Koschnick signed this decree and we were able to proceed.

Clearly the cost was relatively high. After a little study we fixed a total target of DM25 000 per dwelling, and drew up a standard of repair. The numbers were likely to be in hundreds rather than thousands. I decided to take a conventional approach to contracting. Packages of fifteen to thirty houses were defined on the basis of common location. Consultants were hired to prepare a plan and bill of quantities for each house. We then went out to tender and chose the most favourable one—the method is discussed further in Chapter 5. The owner, if known, was requested to sign their approval to the design, and after completion, to sign (along with the Consultant and EUAM Project Manager) to indicate that the contracted works has been completed.

Supervision on site was a task for the consultant architect, but the overall process was controlled by Project Managers in the Reconstruction Department. For rural houses, they were Leif Åmli (from Norway) and Ozrenko Gačić; and for urban houses, Hasan Čemalović. Few people understood the extreme complexity of this task, due particularly to the huge number of separate buildings and owners. Some owners were extremely aggressive and demanding; some builders were lax, but cases of poor performance were often due to objective problems such as the non-availability of components meeting international norms. The general standard was usually good and all projects were satisfactorily completed. Appendix One contains a summary of the data on medium and heavy damage house repair contracts.

Apartment Block Repair Programme

Many of the apartment blocks in east Mostar (and a few in the west) were damaged to a medium or heavy extent. Those with medium damage, such as Maršala Tita Street, 82, were partly inhabited, and cost between DM150 and DM200 per square metre to repair, whereas those with heavy damage, such as Alexa Šantića Street, 4, were wholly uninhabited and cost between DM450 and 500 per square metre.

The maximum cost was about DM25 000 for a three-bedroom apartment. This is arguably a high cost. The World Bank was certainly surprised that we were willing to spend so much on the repair of one dwelling. In 1996, they fixed a maximum budget of DM3000 to repair apartments, but they tackled only the roof and external walls of buildings with low damage levels. No interior repairs, water, sanitary or electrical work was eligible.

Andreas Seebacher argues in Chapter 7 that the people would have carried out this work themselves and that it was wasteful for us to do it. On the other hand, people will not use their own money to repair a flat if the legal ownership is held by another. Also, in a large apartment block, many elements are common, such as lifts, foyers and stairs, and much of the water supply and electrical system. In the situation then obtaining, we could not have got the impoverished inhabitants to cooperate in such tasks, nor could they have afffforded to do so. As regards water supply and sanitation, there was also a public health dimension, and my medical colleagues were very worried about the spread of disease. Many basements were flooded with raw sewage and this was infiltrating the water supply.

Another factor was the psychological and political dimension. I had criticised the Administrator for his decision to rebuild Carinski Bridge to its original Austro-Hungarian design at a cost of DM5 million. I said a Bailey Bridge would suffice. He listened politely, but stuck to his view. At the opening ceremony, I saw I was wrong. The bridge became a symbol of both hope and continuity. It was visually stunning and a tremendous affirmation of the faith of Europe. I mention this, because the repair of many large apartment blocks in Central Mostar to a pristine condition had a similar psychological effect and this was invaluable for the EUAM in terms of its political mission.

But the strongest argument is that we created dwelling space which was not occupied and therefore added to the total stock. This cannot be done for DM3000. No refugees could return to an overcrowded city unless the available habitable space expanded. Appendix One summarises the data on the apartment repair contracts carried through by the EUAM.

The projects were implemented by the method described in Chapter 5. There was an additional problem, however. In occupied or partly occupied blocks, the residents were sometimes in conflict with the builders, whose operations obstructed the normal processes of domestic life. In early projects, this became a nightmare. Builders were obstructed, and I realised that they had a legal basis to claim for indirect loss and expense against the EUAM. We did not have the staff resources to liase properly between the various parties. Stressed housewives with screaming babies occasionally threw builders' equipment out of the window, and at least one workman was seriously injured. I therefore asked the public housing agencies to play a community liaison role. Their staff were paid far less than my staff, and they knew this job better than we did. We paid a one per cent fee and I reckon it was good value. As a result, these socially intricate operations were completed on time, within budget and without hassle.

Projects to Repair Component Systems

We also undertook various repairs to component systems in dwellings which were not otherwise badly damaged. These included:

- lift repairs in high buildings;
- roof repair, flat and pitched;
- communal heating repair;
- electrical and sanitation system repair; and
- window and door repair.

Finally, using modest funds from US Aid, we repaired and re-equipped several children's playgrounds. The contract data are listed in Appendix One.

The lift repair contract was negotiated directly with Končar, which was the original manufacturer in all cases and one of only two such firms in former Yugoslavia —the other being now in Serbia. My staff had no specialist expertise, and moreover we could not protect our interests by competition, so we appointed the consultancy firm Zagrebinspekt to check documents, negotiate prices, inspect works and commission the equipment. After the project, all high apartment buildings had operational lifts. It was part of the contract that Končar should maintain the lifts for five years, since to expend so much money without regular maintenance would be foolish.

Many apartment blocks, whilst fundamentally sound, had damaged roofs, and this was leading to gradual deterioration during the winter time. We set up nine contracts to re-roof both flat and pitched roofs. These were supervised by the municipal technical offices acting as consultants under contract to the EUAM.

In the former Yugoslavia, as in many parts of eastern Europe, new housing areas were heated by communal boiler houses. We repaired several of these systems. To manage these projects, I appointed Zijo Kreso, a mechanical engineer who had managed the Soko aircraft factory before the war. We were concerned that the operating costs, including fuel and maintenance, would not be affordable. We therefore calculated the annual cost per household, and proved that it was indeed affordable. The authorities promised to collect this from the occupiers, and also to maintain the system and supply fuel. As a result of these contracts, dwellings had their heating restored. Regrettably we ran out of time before the full programme could be completed. Part of the original aim had been to reduce electricity consumption. From March 1995, power was restored, but heating requirements in winter threatened to overload the system.

The programme to reglaze windows and provide doors was in part related to the heating repair programme, for obvious reasons. Technisches Hilfswerk signed a contract with us to supply materials and labour, both to cut glass to size and to install it. About 32 000 square metres were supplied during late 1995 and 1996.

Finally, we undertook the repair of electrical systems, water supply and sanitary fittings in the Tekija district during late 1994 and early 1995. This had been identified as a threat to health and a source of fire danger to otherwise habitable and indeed overcrowded apartment blocks.

Conclusion

All these projects were directed by a housing committee, which met weekly under my chairmanship. My staff as well as municipal officials and consultants attended. Just before Christmas 1996 we held the last meeting and a small reception afterwards to thank the numerous co-workers. We had met 120 times, executed 44 contracts, and repaired 6500 houses with 35 000 beneficiaries, expending a total of DM40 million. Everyone had worked tremendously hard under trying circumstances. I believe that all felt a great sense of pride at this extraordinary result.

Chapter 7

The Work of *Technisches Hilfswerk* in Housing Repair

ANDREAS SEEBACHER

Note by John Yarwood

The German federal emergency organisation Technisches Hilfswerk (THW) *was working in Mostar before the EU arrived. It undertook many tasks, with varying degrees of success, but, in my opinion, its most outstanding contribution was the procurement and delivery of building materials to many thousands of damaged properties. Its staff worked with an extremely high level of skill and dedication. No words from me can adequately praise them. For me, and I think also for the people of east Mostar, the staff of THW are real heroes.*

I signed several contracts with THW. The reconstruction agencies of the east municipal council had the task of choosing houses, scheduling work and materials, and organising labour sub-contracts, whereas THW supplied the scheduled material. The EUAM project manager was architect Vladimir Petrović.

When I asked Andreas Seebacher to contribute his views, I realised that he would make points critical of the EU. There is no harm in that, and I add notes at the end of the chapter to comment on controversial points.

In April 1994, Technisches Hilfswerk (Technical Relief Agency), a German governmental organisation working in the field of disaster relief, started its second mission in Mostar. The first mission had been interrupted by the second war in 1993. This was four months before the establishment of the EUAM. The goals were the reconstruction of water and electricity supply systems and schools, the removal of garbage and debris, and, most important of all, the supply of building materials to the city. Their achievement was possible only due to the concerted efforts of THW staff in Bonn as well as Mostar.

The first months were breathless. Everybody in Mostar faced one question: 'where, in heaven, shall we start to work?' The most important success of the early coordination meetings was to define pragmatically the targets and to start with a common effort to realise them. The coordination among the international organisations avoided detrimental competition, reduced the likelihood of double payment for the same project and was a forum for the aid workers to cope with their own emotional problems. Through these meetings ideas emerged about new ways to help achieve our common goal.

We tried to find a 'weighted balance' on both sides of the city, east and west, taking into account the respective degree of destruction and need. Decisive factors were both the benefit for the reunification process (to which we hoped to contribute), and the ratio between the number of inhabitants and the area of inhabitable space.

This chapter concentrates on the repair of buildings and flats covered by two different programmes. One programme, subdivided into several phases, dealt with the distribution of building materials to families, to allow the repair of their dwellings. Approximately 3700 families were helped in this way between August 1994 and August 1996. The other one, the so-called 'ad hoc measure programme', tackled a great variety of interventions and covered approximately 2800 cases.

The opinions expressed here are the author's own and may not reflect the policy of THW.

A Typical Day

Two architects and one logistician from Germany, plus approximately 40 local employees (drivers, workers, interpreters, secretaries and loaders) worked in the field of building material distribution. A typical working day in our warehouse follows.

Early in the morning, one of our bigger trucks, loaded with roofing tiles, cement and electrical parts, travelled from our main base, which was situated some 20 kilometres outside the city, to the warehouse in Mostar. This was located at the tobacco factory, where THW had rented a hall and much of the outdoor space. From here all parts of the city could easily be reached. The truck would be unloaded and then return to the main base, shuttling materials in this way for the whole day. Meanwhile, numerous small trucks would be filled with material in accordance with the orders of our warehouse chief loaders, who were in charge of the delivery papers. These consisted of data on the beneficiary and a bill of quantities. The papers were produced by technicians from the city administration and controlled by EUAM Project Managers and the THW engineers. Larger quantities were loaded by forklift and smaller ones by hand. Sand and gravel (bulk goods) as well as glass, windows and doors were listed on separate papers and dealt with by different working and transport teams, but remained nevertheless part of the total delivery to the beneficiary.

The trucks could enter and leave both hall and warehouse areas through two separate gates. This was important, because even during peak times the distribution process could not be interrupted or slowed down. The smaller goods (nails, wire, putty) were prepared by a special group and handed over to the truck drivers. Once fully loaded, the small trucks would head for the city centre to their destination through sometimes extremely narrow streets.

Soon, all the required materials would be stocked on the beneficiary's site. The rafters would be pulled up to the roof immediately. After this, during a short break for coffee, cigarettes and the obligatory *loza* (schnaps), the owner would sign a receipt for the goods. Back to the warehouse: three more trips, maybe more, then all the workers would have a communal breakfast. Discussions would take place between the German experts and the chief loaders to coordinate their next tasks. This would include discussions with beneficiaries, too, who would come to find out about their own deliveries. From dawn till dusk it would go on like this, seven days a week.

Warehousing

THW had rented two large storage areas. The main base was some 20 kilometres outside the city on Croat-Bosnian territory, while the distribution base was inside the Muslim-controlled eastern part of the city. THW ran its programme for the distribution of building material to families in east Mostar only, though other activities covered the whole city. Although we had planned to work in the city as a whole—and had been asked to do so by the west-side housing authorities—this proved impossible. The reason for this was that the political leaders did everything they could to resist free movement and positive political development in the city. This ranged from permanent political obstruction to open rioting and acts of terrorism. They wanted a separate system for each side. This would have duplicated THW's structure, its facilities, doubling the number of vehicles, and machines, including the acquisition of new trucks, forklifts, excavators etc. This was neither financially nor politically feasible, because it would have signified a premature *de facto* recognition of the separation of the city.

It was a sound strategic decision to have a base warehouse outside the city. This base (at Blizanci), covering approximately 6000 square metres, had a much greater capacity than the one inside the city. This was very important at those times when Mostar was being repeatedly shelled by Serb artillery. No shipping agency was ready to put its goods and vehicles at risk. During the early days most of our suppliers were Croats because in the Muslim-controlled territory production and transport were almost impossible. In addition, for 'political' reasons, some companies did not want or did not dare to cross the border and deliver their goods directly to the warehouse in east Mostar. Another advantage of the external base was the geographical separation of the main office from the field of action. The housing programmes brought with them a huge crowd of clients who would have hampered the normal functioning of our office.

Priorities and Criteria

Some of the priorities for our activities resulted from the guidelines of our organisation. Other criteria had to be defined in conjunction with Mostar authorities and the EU. Others were laid down in the Memorandum of Understanding. At the beginning, we dealt exclusively with lightly damaged houses, in order to have a wide effect on the situation. In this way a larger number of houses could be repaired and more people could benefit from the same amount of money. 'Damage category one' (up to 30 per cent damage) was chosen as the upper limit. This initially sounds reasonable, but becomes somewhat unclear if one examines the definition of the categories and the method of selecting beneficiaries.

It is important to get the social balance right by careful selection of beneficiaries. In view of the financial means, which were small compared with the damage inflicted by the war, it was unavoidable that judgement had to be exercised in the selection of beneficiaries. Among those who took precedence were the elderly and the ill, pregnant and single women with children and families with handicapped members. A minimum repair standard for living space and for bathroom and kitchen facilities had been defined. However, the local authorities insisted on including among the potential beneficiaries war invalids and families who had lost members. This created a problem, because humanitarian aid was used as a kind of war compensation and indemnification payment. For the war invalids, it had the effect of legitimising and justifying their claim for help, independent of the structural repair that their houses actually needed. At the same time other people did not get the help they needed despite their desperate living conditions.

THW wanted a 'help for self-help' approach—it would distribute basic building materials to the flats and houses without expecting to have to pay for the labour. For financial reasons, average values and upper limits had to be determined for the aid available. The programme did not distinguish between private and public property, nor between owners and tenants.

The local administration faced a giant technical and administrative task, but it seemingly wasted a lot of time in argument between local political interests rather than addressing real needs. The EUAM, from my point of view, was a bit too cautious in this regard. Both sides had the advantage of hiding behind a third party (THW) in the case of failure.[1]

In summer 1994, one question dominated the agenda of many meetings: what should be the total value of material delivered to any one beneficiary? We examined several representative bills of quantities of houses for which material had already been brought, and recommended an approximate average value of DM1500 and an upper limit of DM2000. This in reality meant only carrying out emergency repair work and did not aim to cover the full 30 per cent loss of value of the building. Experience showed that the definition of a maximum value was of great importance, because otherwise many single low value 'contracts' (e.g. DM50 for glass panes) could have been offset against one very expensive repair. 'Contract' was the expression used for the bill of quantity, according to which beneficiaries' entitlement to materials was worked out. This term resulted from the quasi-contractual obligation between THW and the beneficiaries. The real contracts were obviously signed between THW, EUAM and the local administration. In principle, a quick, rough survey of all war damage in the city was necessary in order to identify which properties had only been lightly damaged. Only then should buying of material have started. Such a rigorous survey had been done—after some delay—but due to the politics of the area, a systematic approach to choosing beneficiaries had been rejected.

The degree of damage could vary considerably. There were cases where only window panes had to be replaced. In other cases, the whole roof, walls or internal installations were missing. Historic buildings had often been completely destroyed by the shelling and by fire. Also, there were different causes of damage. Besides war damage, plundering, vandalism and, most of all, weather had caused sometimes severe secondary damage. The houses had been exposed for two winters to rain and theft. Even though our programme obviously aimed at the alleviation of war damage and not at that caused by the natural ageing of buildings, it was unreasonable to distinguish between the two. Neither could we limit the range of materials we supplied. For example, in the beginning we did not deliver water boilers or the associated cables. But not delivering this cable would cause problems later on, when the beneficiaries were obliged to break up their walls to install them. This meant they had to wait for all materials to be supplied before starting work, delaying our programme and running contrary to our aims. Gradually, as we discussed the progress of our reconstruction programme, we increased the number of items on our supply list, thus broadening the scope of the distribution process. Each new item added to the list increased the number of ancillary parts we needed to supply to allow for its installation. There was some reluctance to add extra items because, for example, the cost of one electrical 10-litre boiler (plus connection parts) corresponded to 16 square metres of roofing tiles, or eight square metres of repaired wall (20 cm thick with plaster) or one new window (iso-glazed, 80×90 cm). And roofs, walls and windows definitely had a higher priority than a boiler, especially if one counts the benefit of a repaired roof on a multi-storey building for all its occupants. We were forced to make compromises, because the city's rehabilitation process progressed much faster than anybody would have thought in 1994. To hinder this process would have been counter-productive. Despite this, we tried to strike a balance between higher standards for the few people and a wide spread of benefits for the many.

The Ad Hoc Programme

The second of our programmes, the so-called *ad hoc* programme, covered the whole of Mostar and was certainly very effective. One reason behind this programme was the many cases that could not be covered by formal contracts, due to their urgency or small scale. These cases ranged from the repair of the city's pharmacy or a bakery to the delivery of a few wooden planks and nails for a coffin or a beehive or the renovation of the university canteen kitchen. Such rapid help also acted as a kind of moral support, especially during times of shelling. Just an hour after a grenade had exploded in the city, the damage had been surveyed, and the day after the material was delivered. The programme had started with spontaneous donations from abroad and was run part-time by THW engineers in parallel with their other work. Later, the EUAM reserved a separate fund, and THW employed a full time engineer.

From a central financial reserve, THW crew members could provide assistance in accordance with certain criteria. These were:

- the repair of living space;
- the creation of income and food production;
- the relief of extreme social burdens;
- the repair of social and cultural infrastructure; and, of course
- social need (which could be easily checked by interview).

Up to a defined limit, THW had the discretion to implement the aid itself. Amounts that went beyond the limit had to be countersigned by EUAM officials. Every citizen could ask for this help, as well as local officials, companies, relief organisations and—last but not least—the EUAM itself. Within the framework of this programme, we were exceptionally allowed to finance labour. This was useful in those cases where THW was trying to get old people out of the dank basements where they had been living under terrible conditions. We asked the local authorities to indicate those buildings in which, once repaired by our labour team, several elderly people could live.

Political Conflict

Humanitarian aid had a political importance for the donors, and this was also reflected at the local level. Soon after summer 1994, the SDA (the 'Party of Democratic Action' that held power at the time) replaced all staff in important positions within the local administration with its own functionaries. They politicised all humanitarian aid by passing it off as their own. This was easy because the SDA decided who could benefit from such aid. From the outset, the understanding was that the local administration would be in charge of choosing the beneficiaries, because they had a better knowledge of the population structure. This behaviour, together with a number of nasty incidents, caused us to stop for a while the processing of these *ad hoc* requests for aid from local officials. Those applications made by individuals and international officials were dealt with normally.

The payment of taxes and salaries received lengthy discussion among the relief organisations. The demand (both in west and east Mostar) to pay taxes for 'importing' humanitarian aid was regarded by many relief organisations as arrogant abuse, even though it could be avoided by operating through the EUAM which was free of tax obligations. Regarding the payment of employees, the main difficulty was in the comparability of salary levels, because doctors, teachers, administrative officials and others received their remuneration only in the form of food. That everybody had to pay taxes on the salaries (even from humanitarian aid) was an understandable regulation. But for THW the competition from the black labour market was problematic. Working on the black market resulted in higher profits when private—and less controlled—money was involved, mostly paid by people with family members abroad.

In general we had good contacts with the local administration, but we received little help from it in our search for appropriate storage facilities. On the contrary, the rental levels for warehouse premises were horrific. Another concern for our local employees was the lack of cooperation from the local authorities. Some of them were transferred to the front line and replaced by workers chosen by the local administration. That meant we could only recruit workers from among those who were not subject to army obligations—in other words, we were limited to older people, whose years of experience quickly proved able to compensate for their slower working speed. Nevertheless, we maintained our support for the few workers we had who were subject to army obligations, as they had been recruited before this issue had arisen. We were afraid of lasting negative consequences if we showed weakness, and also that our new recruits might not be so loyal towards THW. We had genuine reasons for such worries. The most flagrant case was surely the forcible removal of files from our office, committed by the acting chief of the 'Commission for War Damage Evaluation'. Besides that, our younger employees provided the link between the German expatriate experts and the warehouse workers and, had we lost them, we would also have lost the experience and confidence they had so far built up. The repeated conscription of our qualified workers threatened the success of our work to such a degree that we closed down in protest. Of course, neither could we tolerate those employees who worked in our services for their own financial gain. After appropriate warnings they were fired, as to do otherwise would have seriously damaged our reputation.

Procurement of Materials

Several times the east Mostar authorities tried to influence the way we bought building materials. Their interest was that we bought more material in territory under Muslim control. We proceeded according to European norms by choosing from at least three tenders for precisely defined goods the one with the best price-quality ratio. Here, the time factor played an important role because of the urgency of our task. The local authorities negotiated with Mr Koschnick a clause that allowed THW to exceed by 10 per cent the best offer in favour of an offer from suppliers in a Muslim-controlled area. It soon became clear that this was not practical because of the damage caused to production capacities and transportation difficulties. More and more, the increasing demand for such products in the country became a problem. Materials were ordered from other European countries during the early stages of the programme, when hardly any goods could be found in Bosnia Hercegovina itself. Later on, only specialised materials and products in short supply were bought outside the country. It was one of THW's aims to buy as much as possible in the country itself in order to stimulate the local economy. But there were two more reasons for purchasing goods and materials inside Bosnia: the lower transportation costs and the reluctance of foreign shipping agencies to send goods and vehicles to an area rocked by civil war.

We set up a 'list of guide prices for materials', which allowed us to quickly evaluate tenders and estimate the value of distributed materials. Together with the purchase bills and delivery specifications, attested through signature by beneficiaries upon receipt, it became part of the final accounting system which we presented to donors. The 'guide prices' helped steer a course between the ever-present perils of inflation and deflation, between accountability to the local authorities, the beneficiaries and the clients, and finally between planned figures and realised cases. Additionally, the list took on a city-wide importance during the first twelve months, because both companies and local officials used it in making their own calculations. Other humanitarian organisations also used these indicative prices. Incoming relief agencies did not have to accept excessive price levels. Since material and labour costs were usually in a ratio of 1:1, the list was important, too, for organisations that paid for both.

Some material donations from German companies proved rather embarrassing for us, being geared more towards clearing their warehouses in Germany than humanitarian engagement in Bosnia-Hercegovina; how else could the sending of, for example, expensive spare parts for vacuum cleaners be explained? In this context I would like to stress that used material in good condition was in principle of great use and was often used to great advantage, as beneficiaries did not have to include it in official bills of quantities.

Local Perceptions of our Motive

Often THW was perceived by local people as a 'company'. Our employees liked to speak about 'their company'. They certainly drew parallels with their pre-war jobs, and THW obviously had more workers over a much longer period than any other humanitarian organisation in Mostar. It had many employees, machines and vehicles, marked by their dark blue colour, all over the city. We had pumped huge amounts of materials into the city. But this view of our role had serious disadvantages. Commercial contractors would usually have taken on paid work for money without philosophical objections. In the opinion of some Mostarians, the EUAM money had become their own property from the day that the organisation had been set up. But THW's remit was to work on a non-profit, cost-recovery basis according to certain philosophical principles. Our purchase orders were carried out according to strict rules, and very soon the private companies came to understand that that was how we operated. But for some time it did not occur to local politicians that THW was not like a commercial contractor—a paid recipient of orders from the powerful.

'Cuckoo's Eggs'

Our materials distribution procedure was repeatedly hampered and altered, not only by political interference but also on a technical level. Sometimes extremely badly prepared bills of quantities ('contracts') listed the wrong types and amounts of materials. This situation did not improve after the local administration received payment from the EUAM for the technical survey, thus enabling them to take on more staff. The only conclusion we could draw was that the data they contained had been deliberately changed.

Two notable cases should be mentioned. A high ranking army officer put in a claim for materials worth several thousand German Marks, while in reality the only damage to his house was a pistol shot through one window pane. The repair bill for the house of an administrative official who was in charge of assigning army duties, came in at DM10 000. With this money he hoped to build a high-standard flat in his attic. The actual damage was below DM15: some broken roofing tiles! These and other such cases could be weeded out and eliminated through random checking mostly aimed at those 'contracts' with a high material value. Of course there are no reliable data about these 'cuckoo's eggs', but we estimate that the proportion was around 20 to 25 per cent. This may seem high, but approximately 10 per cent of cases, though not fulfilling all official criteria, involved rebuilding houses or flats, thus adding to the total amount of inhabitable space. Only around 10 per cent of the materials we supplied went to recipients interested in re-selling them on the black market. This is a very low rate, bearing in mind the post-war situation, and even here, it still served to bring new building material into the city! In spite of all our efforts to limit such abuse, it was impossible to exclude it completely. Only a huge increase in bureaucracy could have achieved that aim, but this would have seriously damaged our efforts to be a rapid response 'task force'.

Distribution of Material

Often materials could not be distributed because of supply failure due to production and security problems. But sometimes materials were specified that exceeded agreed standards and were not part of our range. This was due to a long lasting conflict over repair standards caused by local politicians' unrealistic promises. Sometimes there was insufficient space at a beneficiary's site to accommodate all the materials they required, leading to several, more expensive deliveries. Storing materials on public ground worked quite well due to the high level of social control in the city. Materials that were reported stolen were never replaced as such theft could not be verified. We also never reimbursed people who claimed to have previously borrowed building material and asked THW to return it to its proper owner. We would otherwise have risked an avalanche of similar claims. Also, no material was sent in cases that would have compromised the historical quality of the city centre by altering the appearance of old buildings (e.g. the provision of red clay roofing tiles to people who wanted to replace their old white lime slate tiles). Poor water and electricity supply also hampered the success of our work. But more importantly, many men were still under obligation to the army and had to be excluded from the programme as 'self-helpers'. Also, uncertainty about where the sporadic mortar attacks would hit next discouraged people from starting to use the materials we had distributed.

We tried to maintain standards of quality when ordering materials and also by carefully checking supplies as they arrived. On several occasions we rejected complete truck-loads. Some supply companies ended up on an internal 'black list'. We had repeatedly been blackmailed into buying material in Muslim-controlled areas. For example, we used to distribute sand bought in an area which was under Croat control. Under pressure from the east Mostar authorities, we started using their sand which was of very poor quality. To ward off the complaints of beneficiaries, we could of course justifiably lay the blame at the door of local administration, but the absurdity of the situation meant that, at the end of the day, we had to bear the brunt of any failings which arose.

Controversy over Standards of Repair

A building's roof is important due to the protection it offers from the elements and because of its cultural importance. So it came as no surprise to find that many people repaired the roof first, often using improvised materials. Despite this, we regrettably never managed to convince either the local authorities or the EUAM to agree to a programme that would deal only with roofs (including the supporting walls and chimneys) and with the outer skin (walls, windows and doors). Proposals to this effect were regarded as insufficient, and there were also disagreements within THW on this point. But an experiment demonstrated that such a programme would have been well received. Within the framework of the *ad hoc* programme we put a new roof on a big building containing some 600 square metres of usable space on four floors. At that time only two parties lived in the basement and a section of the ground floor. Vulnerable to the elements, the rest of the building was unoccupied. A short time after the new roof was completed, two more families moved in on the ground floor, and the two upper floors were settled later. Today this building is home to twelve families. All newcomers had to provide their own doors, windows etc.

A 'roofing and wall programme' had several aims. First, concentrating on the most important parts of the building would have reduced the amount of material required per house or family, so that more people could have benefited from the materials supplied. Second, it would have limited the scope for abuse of the system. Third, it would have given a boost to private initiative, which remained dormant as long as people could count on humanitarian aid. Fourth, it would have reduced the range of items supplied and therefore storage costs. And monitoring would have been easier. Sixthly, it would have raised fewer problems with repatriation and the related issues of ownership.

But such a reduction in the quality of humanitarian aid (which the local politicians promised to their population and took credit for themselves) would have reflected badly on these politicians. Politicians and administrators found it easier and politically more lucrative to help those individuals who carried the most influence. Mindful of their high pre-war standard of living, the population's expectations of us were equally high. In addition the leading political party was quite confident that it would win the forthcoming election. Any failings in the materials supply programme could easily be blamed on the foreign donors. And a great many of the homeless, as newcomers to the city, having been displaced from their home town, had virtually no say in the running of Mostar. It was not only political aspirations that caused 'mistakes', but often genuine fear. Local officials were exposed to popular pressure, ranging from verbal to physical or even armed attacks, including threats to their families.

The EUAM was understandably interested in producing impressive tangible results, which could be shown to both the population in Mostar and to the international media. But I regret that this meant the exclusion of a 'roof-and-wall programme'.[2] Part of the discrepancy resulted from the fact that the THW goal was to provide emergency aid, while the EUAM mandate consisted of a more comprehensive reconstruction programme.

Certainly, THW should have reacted earlier than it did to its one main shortcoming: the 'self-help' idea fell short of one of its basic preconditions, namely the availability of labour. For much of the time, the men required to make the programme successful were abroad, at the front line or in hospital (or dead). Old people, women and children could not compensate for the lack of manpower and technical knowledge. Solidarity among neighbours might have been strong during the war, but it decreased rapidly, as living conditions improved. I mention this because THW had based its strategy on self-help, and problems in this quarter caused delays in achieving programme results. THW should have employed a labour force from the outset, despite the fact that this would cause problems when labour was reduced at a later date. Yet another problem at that time was the fact that companies in Mostar were often composed of nothing but a name, a director and a secretary, while companies from other cities were unwilling to come to Mostar due to security problems.

Conclusion

Maybe we cared too little about public relations. It might seem strange under civil war circumstances, but the nature of our operations required more public information about THW. People in Mostar felt insecure when faced with the flood of unknown names like 'EUAM', 'ICRC', 'UNPROFOR', 'THW' and others, because their intentions were not made clear. A formal introduction (and regular explanations of purpose via the radio) would have been good for THW, to show what its aims, methods and limitations were. This would have helped to counteract the attitude of some politicians and prevent them from using THW for their own ends.

We got strong, positive feedback and support from Mostar's population. At first this was a delicate matter for us as a German governmental organisation. We were afraid that some degree of historically founded resentment might arise. But this feedback helped us a lot, too, when things went wrong and motivation was low.

The German government itself interfered with our work, placing restrictions on us that made our task more difficult and exposed us to some degree of ridicule. Not more than three German experts were allowed to be in the city at the same time, and never during the night. Also we could not leave the Mostar area in the direction of central Bosnia. Sometimes we were forced to break these rules at our own risk. The German government wanted to avoid negative newspaper headlines about the possible dangers in a country where—for reasons related to domestic policy—it had long planned to deploy its army. Looking back, I really regret the overly strong influence of local and international politics over humanitarian aid. This viewpoint might seem naive, but can be understood when viewed through the eyes of an aid worker faced daily by the horrors and misery of the war.

I would like to emphasise the social aspect of THW's working philosophy. Old or sick people, widows with children and displaced persons were without a lobby, and THW could help them through its work. Fighting for social ideas meant fighting for equal rights and thus necessarily provoking the opposition of those who had come to power. Correct administration endangered their dominion. Our lives could definitely have been easier. The balancing act between 'being a guest' and the mandate of bringing humanitarian aid was a difficult one—but it was worth it!

NOTES BY JOHN YARWOOD

1 Seebacher refers here to our friendly disagreement on payment for labour and consultancy. He wished to devote all EUAM finance to materials, and to distribute less per case. But I believed that labour, whether manual or expert, could only be motivated by proper contracts and payment at market rates. He also felt that I was too 'soft' in my dealings with local politicians, and made too many compromises in order to get their cooperation. He wanted THW or EUAM to control more closely the choice of beneficiaries. But I came to believe that this should be done by the authorities who were in *de facto* control of their communities. We could have done little without their cooperation and it was self-defeating for us to derogate from their authority at grass-roots level during a time of post-war chaos. I completely respected and admired the THW position, but felt it was unrealistic. Perhaps this illustrates the contrast between German rigour and idealism on the one hand, and the British tendency to pragmatic—or, if you prefer, sloppy—compromise on the other. We set up a computerised system for financial control and monitored cases closely. This avoided abuse

(after a few early scandals). It would have been fatal to get locked into conflict with partners whose cooperation was critical for success. I tried to be reasonable and practical but increasingly strict on matters of principle. In the end, the Court of Auditors could discover no laxity of control or sustained abuse.

2 Notwithstanding this statement by Andreas, many thousands of houses were repaired under EUAM contracts at very low cost—for example, the first two contracts allowed DM1500 for materials and DM500 for labour. This covered 3500 houses—no more than just roof and walls. On later contracts, I increased the budget to allow for water and electricity connections, since a house is hard to inhabit without them. Self-help was not such a practical possibility. We also aimed to resuscitate the economy, of which the construction sector was a leading part.

Chapter 8

Health, Education and Other Building Projects

This chapter records all building projects other than housing. There is also a general discussion of political issues which impacted upon the programme and our ability to realise it.

Health Buildings

Fifteen health buildings, all heavily damaged, were repaired and medically re-equipped to a high standard. In several cases, this involved major new works to extend the existing facilities. Five health buildings were completely new structures, namely the 'Dom Zdravlja' hospital, the east old persons' home and three local clinics. The contract details are scheduled in Appendix One.

These projects fall into four categories:

- seven local clinics, known as 'ambulantas', which served neighbourhoods or nearby villages, providing primary health care;
- two old people's homes, one on each side;
- three hospitals, including a general hospital on the east side ('South Camp') and also one on the west side ('Dom Zdravlja'), as well as a paediatric and maternity hospital ('Brankovac'); and
- three support facilities, namely the public health institute, social work centre and rehabilitation centre.

The EUAM Director of Health, Dr Pasqualino ('Nino') Procacci, managed the implementation of the construction projects. I interviewed and selected several Bosnian architects (at his request) and they worked under his general guidance. Upon his departure in July 1996, the responsibility was passed to me and his staff joined the Reconstruction Department.

In addition to his medical experience, Dr Procacci was a knowledgeable health systems planner. He commissioned Italian consultants to prepare a careful review of the existing situation and to propose a rational plan for the future. This covered all aspects of the health system, such as organisation and management, manpower and training, equipment and drugs, and finance. The aim was to repair the system itself—not just physical objects—but he did not succeed altogether. The reason for this was, I suspect, once again, the reluctance of the EUAM to take a systems perspective.

I will also mention the politics of health. Mostar had had one major general hospital at Bijeli Brijeg. This was on Croat territory. Mr Koschnick wanted to press the Croats to admit Muslim patients and doctors, so that once again it would become a facility for the entire sub-region. The Croats would not agree, and we held out against them for a long time. The improvised hospital facilities in east Mostar—the so-called Velmos Hospital—were disgusting, and the Muslim side accused us of doing nothing. Late in the day, therefore, we decided to create a separate hospital for the east at South Camp. This made Bijeli Brijeg less than viable and we were persuaded still later to build a new small hospital (Dom Zdravlja) in the west.

This was contrary to the political objective of unification, but was justified on humanitarian grounds. Action was postponed through a long period of negotiation, led by Dr Procacci, on freedom of movement of doctors and patients. This disrupted the logic and timing of the original programme.

The EUAM project managers working on health building projects were Jelica Rašeta-Jurišić, Zvonimir Petričević and Mevludin Zečević.

Education Projects

The following is contributed by the former EUAM Director of Education, Dr Hedwig Wolfram. The editor adds some observations of his own at the end.

The Department of Education and Culture was directed from September 1994 until July 1995 by Mr Helmut Bachmann, Headmaster of the Agricultural Secondary School in Kematen, Tyrol, Austria, and from September 1995 until July 1996 by Dr Hedwig Wolfram, Ambassador (retired) from the Austrian Ministry for External Affairs.

The Department dealt with the rehabilitation of schools, kindergartens and cultural institutions along with the preservation of historical buildings. Construction projects represented about 95 per cent of the Department's activities; about five per cent concerned contacts between teachers and pupils from Mostarian schools with schools abroad. The Department was involved in the realisation of 59 projects, 54 of which were carried out entirely under the Department's responsibility.

As far as schools are concerned, the reconstruction programme was more than fulfilled. The aim was to restore all the elementary schools within the boundary. In fact, four secondary schools and nine schools outside the boundary were also restored. Only one elementary school on the west side, School No. 3, remained unrepaired as it was so heavily damaged that reconstruction was impossible. The administration had envisaged building a new School No. 3; but after the attacks on the Administrator's car in February 1996, this plan was cancelled.

In autumn 1994, there were about 12 000 children of school age in Mostar who, after an interruption of two years, needed to go to school as soon as possible. As practically all the schools in the area had been damaged during the wars by shelling, fighting or vandalism, it was the administration's first aim in the field of education to restore all elementary schools. The works started with the greatest possible speed.

Generally speaking, there were three waves of school restorations. The first wave covered 12 elementary schools in Mostar and started in September 1994. These schools were finished during the spring/summer of 1995. The second wave, which covered eight schools inside and outside the EUAM boundary line, started around July 1995. These schools were finished between the end of 1995 and spring 1996. The third wave again covered eight schools. As new projects were stopped for political reasons between the middle of January and the end of March 1996, these projects were started in May/June 1996 and were finished during July/August of that year.

Until spring 1995, the administration abstained from restoring secondary schools because there was no freedom of movement between the two parts of the city. Integrated schooling with free access to all secondary schools for all children from both sides of the Neretva was impossible. However, the EUAM considered integrated schooling to be a precondition for the repair of the secondary schools. In early summer 1995, an attempt was made and reconstruction works started in four secondary schools (three in west Mostar and one in east Mostar). As the attitude of the Croats to freedom of movement remained unchanged, work on two schools in west Mostar was again stopped and only two vocational secondary schools were restored during this period.

Altogether 28 buildings accommodating schools were restored, 13 on the east side and 15 on the west side. According to our data, 15 940 pupils attended schools in the Mostar municipality, 7680 on the east side and 8260 on the west side.

Simultaneously with the rehabilitation of schools, the restoration of seven kindergartens and the construction of one new kindergarten was completed. There were four in east Mostar and four in west Mostar. Additionally, a donated container-kindergarten was moved to Mostar and set up at the east side. Around DM25 million was spent on the repair and refurbishment of these schools and kindergartens, of which about DM21 million came through the EUAM and DM4 million as direct contributions by donors.

As far as the rehabilitation of cultural buildings is concerned, five of them were restored: the Archives of Hercegovina, the Children's Library, the City Library (Dom Kulture), the Puppet Theatre (as a multi-purpose hall for theatre and film performances, concerts and seminars) and Dom Kulture in the suburb of Rodoć. Three of them are located on the east side and two on the west side.

Finally, preservation work was undertaken to protect 14 historical buildings (seven on the east side and seven on the west side) from further decay, among them four mosques, the Bishop's Ordinate, the Franciscan Monastery (new roof), the Old Orthodox Church and the Gymnasium No. 1 (new roof). More than DM4 milion was spent on the rehabilitation or preservation of these buildings.

Note by John Yarwood

It is only fair to mention staff by name. Sterling work was done by Gerard Kuiper, a Dutch architect, who managed all education construction projects, and his successors, Andreas Seebacher and Miro Mihič, a local engineer. The speed and efficiency of their work was remarkable. Also, the Director of Cultural Life, Youth and Sports, Oswald Schroeder, carried out wonderfully spirited work on a tiny budget, organising and supporting music, art exhibitions, theatre, youth clubs and sport. He worked at grass-roots level to regenerate the spirit of the people. Given greater (although still modest) resources, he could have done much to achieve our political goals by his 'bottom-up' approach. This can often play a role which complements the 'top-down' methods of the politician or diplomat.

Miscellaneous Projects

Building projects were commissioned from the Reconstruction Department by the Departments of City Administration, Cultural Life, Economy and Transport, and Police. These projects are listed in Appendix One. Project Manager for this task was Abdurezak Abduzaimović, formerly Engineering Director of Unioninvest and one of the most respected architect-engineers in Bosnia. He was assisted by Mrs Dženana Maglajlić-Bijedić, a young architect of great character and ability.

The Hotel Mostar was intended to serve for two years as a hostel for the European Police Force. After a rent-free period, the repaired building was to revert to the owner, the Hetmos hotel company. The office building of the contractor GP Hercegovina was taken over by agreement for two years and repaired as the headquarters of the Unified Police Force.

Key municipal buildings were repaired to allow government functions to restart. These included the Pensions Administration building, the Fire Station, the Municipal Technical Agencies building, the High Court building, the Sutina cemetery, the Jewish cemetery and the Šoinovac cemetery, the Public Works Depot, and the Office of the Institute for Historic Conservation ('Dom Ribara').

A major new municipal project was the solid waste landfill site at Uborak, five kilometres north of the city. This incorporated six specialised subcontracts as follows: (1) earthworks; (2) concrete works; (3) drainage and ventilation works; (4) metalwork; (5) membrane installation; and (6) electrical works. The total value was DM4.4 million, one of our largest projects. The problems of waste disposal in Mostar before the war were serious, and led to pollution of ground water, but with this project the EUAM had solved the problem.

Other projects included the repair of the city cold store (for meat and vegetables); the youth centre; Mostar Airport, the Railway Station; the Bus Station; and a Women's Training Centre (the 'Sumeja' Building). Two large workshop buildings were repaired to provide a base for the construction equipment pool, which is described in Chapter 10. A building on Onescukova Street (in the Old

Town) was repaired as a Technical Training Centre, which the EUAM established (this is also described in Chapter 10). Finally, the Hotel Bristol was repaired to provide temporary accommodation for experts, such as doctors and engineers, who would—we hoped—return from abroad to take up their old jobs once again. After three years, the building would revert to the original owner and begin to function again as a hotel.

Chapter 9

Demolition

NIELS STRUFE

Note by John Yarwood

Central Mostar was a devastated area in 1994. As soon as possible, I invited five specialised consultancy firms to make a submission covering their track-record and approach. In the conditions obtaining, a quick decision was needed and I chose the Danish firm DEMEX, which was managed by a leading demolition and recycling expert, Erik Lauritzen. He proposed a partnership with a structural engineering firm, Rambøll, Hanneman and Højlund. After negotiation we signed a consultancy contract in early 1995. The first problem was the lack of a legal basis for demolition work to buildings which we did not own. Usually, the ownership was in dispute between Croats and Muslims. A decree was drafted to give us the necessary powers, which was signed by the Administrator (after consultation and agreement from both sides) on 19 March 1995.

To set up a comprehensive contract would have taken a long time, so we pursued very quickly a small 'emergency contract' which was awarded to the Scandinavian Demolition Company after an international tender on rates.

The major contract (1995/96) followed on, and Niels Strufe describes this here. It had a tremendous impact on the appearance of the city. Streets had been blocked by masses of fallen masonry. Building interiors were full of rubble. The city was in a horrific mess. Afterwards, of course, ruins were still evident, but they were clean and orderly. Doors and windows were neatly closed, streets were clear, unstable walls were propped by timber scaffolds, and structures exposed to rain were protected from further deterioration. Many buildings were utterly destroyed and incapable of later repair, and these were totally cleared. The most important example was the Razvitak Building on Maršala Tita Street, a nine storey reinforced concrete slab block, built in the 1970s. It was very ugly and its removal greatly improved the skyline.

We also established a waste material sorting, recycling and storage centre. A mobile concrete crushing plant was donated by the Danish Government. This centre employed many people, and the sale of material created an income large enough to sustain its ongoing operation. This was donated to the city prior to the end of the mandate.

This chapter describes a contract for the protection of damaged buildings and waste management in the reconstruction of Mostar. The work was driven by an urgent need to secure the buildings against any hazard posing a threat to human lives and health. The works were carried out between November 1995 and August 1996. The demolition and protection work was sent to international tendering as a single contract in November 1996 and the contract was awarded to Detecsa of Madrid.

We applied the EUAM Decree on Demolition of Building Structures, in close cooperation with the local municipal authorities of Mostar. They also provided the data and information required by the project. The Old Town in Mostar ('Stari Grad') has now been cleaned up and most important buildings of historical and cultural interest have been protected against further damage. Reusable materials were sorted and transported to a suitable repository. The work in Stari Grad was supervised by the Institute for Preservation of Cultural and Historical Heritage.

The original contract comprised 56 buildings with a total built area of 49 099 square metres, though this was reduced during the working period to 51 buildings with a total of 43 198 square metres. A building by the Lućki bridge was added to the contract. The Stari Grad project in the Old Town of Mostar was also added and comprised 42 historical buildings with an area of 4400 square metres. In total, 95 buildings with a built area of 47 798 square metres were included. The protection works were planned and conducted according to engineering designs and approval by those parties involved.

About 5000 square metres of scaffolding were used during the contract, along with 10 000 square metres of reinforcement net and fine mesh net for the proper closing of buildings. The protection work also produced considerable amounts of reusable materials, such as decorative stones, rough cut stones and stone blocks and masonry, which were sorted out on site and reused during the protection work. Remaining reusable materials were stored inside the individual buildings with the intention of using them in connection with future repair and reconstruction work.

Description of Works

The subject of the project was the protection, cleaning and clearing of damaged buildings, including sorting, transport and disposal of reusable and waste materials. This involved the following operations:

- temporary scaffolding;
- partial demolition of unsafe building elements;
- shoring of facades and securing of unstable construction elements;
- cleaning of rubble from inside the buildings;
- closing of supply installations (water, electricity, etc.);
- closing of buildings;
- on-site sorting of waste;
- crushing/cutting of rubble material;
- transportation of reusable material;
- transportation and disposal of waste.

The work was planned and conducted according to an engineering design for each individual building (prepared with respect to future plans for repair and reconstruction). The engineering design by the contractor was based on a detailed survey of structural stability and risk analysis of possible structural failures and collapses, including seismic impact (Mostar is earthquake-prone). Work was principally categorised into three different activities:

- protection (of the heavily damaged buildings category), comprising all kinds of partial demolition and construction work to protect buildings against further destruction and to protect people against the risk of structural collapse and falling objects. This also included the sorting and removal of waste and materials from inside the damaged buildings;
- cleaning (of the heavily damaged buildings category), comprising the sorting and removal of waste and materials from inside these buildings; and
- clearing (of the totally damaged buildings category), comprising the clearing of building structures that posed a risk to the safety of the public. Basements were cleaned of rubble and waste and closed to the public in order to prevent illegal access and rubbish dumping.

The work was carried out under the following general conditions:

- no demolition of bearing structures began unless the remaining structure had been supported and adequate measures had been taken to prevent any accidents from happening; and
- engineering design had to follow appropriate norms and standards given in the technical specifications.

All work was carried out in a way that respected the following general requirements:

- no damage to neighbouring property;
- a minimum of dust, noise, and vibration;
- minimal risk to traffic and people;
- maximum protection of historical buildings;
- maximum attention to be paid to workers' health and safety; and
- cleaning of the site after the work had been completed.

The contractor was fully responsible for all protection against any damage that could have arisen from the work. The contractor was also required to meet costs for any repair and reinstatement work that had to be carried out as a result of its works.

Before any work on a specific building was begun, the contractor carried out a detailed survey of the structure of the building and any adjoining buildings. The structural survey identified the principal supporting elements at each floor, and the inter-dependence of structures that might have affected the sequence and procedure of the works. The structural survey was carried out under the supervision of the contractor's professionally qualified structural engineer. Based on the structural survey and list of buildings, the contractor prepared its engineering design for works to be carried out on the building.

Management of Material and Waste

The management of material and waste comprised the following four main categories:

- reusable materials (roofing tiles, timber, iron, etc.);
- rubble materials (masonry, stones and concrete);
- waste materials (organic waste, paper, plastic, garbage); and
- unexploded ordnance (UXO).

Reusable material was, after on-site sorting, divided into the following categories:

- roofing tiles and plates;
- masonry and quarry stones;
- decorated stones for facades;
- iron works, street lamps, etc.;
- timber, doors, windows and other wooden materials;
- materials for heating systems; and
- scrap metal.

The reusable materials, except scrap metal, were stored inside the original buildings. However, if the building was to be totally demolished, all material was transported and disposed of at the recycling station.

Rubble materials included clean concrete, stone and masonry rubble, sand, grit and soil. It was important that the materials were clean and without any organic content, garbage, wood, etc. which could have polluted the river and the ground water.

Waste materials were disposed of at municipal landfills, as directed by the engineer. This waste included small amounts of asphalt and hazardous materials such as oil and chemicals, asbestos, etc. which require special treatment. Asbestos removal was carried out before the commencement of the contract works. It was packed in sealed bags and transported to the landfill site. Generally, only very small amounts of oil and chemical waste were found. Such waste was packed in sealed bags and disposed of at the landfill.

Military ammunition, unexploded shells and mines, abandoned ammunition and explosives required special treatment. This was provided by the Spanish Army.

Chapter 10

Construction Industry Recovery

It became clear at the beginning that the resources of the construction industry—in terms of equipment, men, and skills (both technical, professional and managerial)—were damaged, and in east Mostar comprehensively destroyed. It seemed to me that if we spent a lot of money on physical repairs in a short time period, and if the work was mainly done by local companies, there would be a serious lack of capacity on the supply side. This would lead to high costs, poor quality and slow performance. A balanced approach therefore required us to enhance capacity as well as boost demand.

In January 1995, after extensive consultations in the industry, I submitted a paper to Mr Koschnick, which argued for several forms of action:

- set up a construction equipment pool and hire out equipment for a fee;
- give loans to construction firms, material producers, builders' merchants and professional offices;
- encourage partnership with foreign firms, including skill transfer and investment;
- support the creation of professional societies and trade associations, particularly, perhaps, technical libraries;
- establish a technical training centre and relate training to specified manpower and skill problems;
- repair (via grants or loans) material production processes, such as quarries, brickworks and joinery workshops;
- repair and re-equip a materials testing laboratory; and
- create a materials procurement and distribution organisation, in partnership with defunct local merchants.

I proposed to give this task to consultants and asked the Crown Agents (the only relevant agency in theatre at the time) to organise this. A short consultancy exercise was undertaken, which was completed in March 1995. The Economy Department took up the administration of grants to builders, although not to materials producers. This led to either imports or to poor quality materials and components. Also, the grants were not given in accordance with any strategy regarding the future pattern of the industry. Nothing was done by the EUAM to improve material procurement, but the German government agency, Technisches Hilfswerk (THW), cancelled its withdrawal plan and in 1995 expanded to fill much of this need. Several initiatives were implemented by the EUAM, however, namely the construction equipment pool, the technical training centre, and the testing laboratory.

Construction Equipment Pool

I tried to persuade my local colleagues to create a single construction equipment pool, with freedom of movement for equipment. At first I thought I was making progress. My Croat co-head, Boro Puljić, attended several meetings in the east, which in late 1994 was a brave gesture. As the idea became more widely known, I believe Croat hardliners clamped down, and in any case the Muslims would by then not trust them to return equipment once on Croat territory. Even a bulldozer was to be either Catholic or Muslim! By summer 1995, it was clear that we would get either two pools or none.

In any case, the objective need lay mainly on the east side. I decided to press ahead on the Muslim side and create a small pool on the west to maintain our reputation for even-handedness. The result was that the west pool was so small that its commercial viability was marginal.

I asked Crown Agents to find an expert to execute the task, and they nominated Dick Mills, who proved to be excellent in every way. We met with experts from both sides to agree a list of equipment (which is summarised in Appendix One). The Crown Agents procured this by international tender according to EU regulations—an enormously complex task which we could not have done ourselves. Even so, some German colleagues opposed the project because they feared British manufacturers would be favoured. They told me that since Germany contributed so large a proportion of the EU budget, they could not accept Crown Agents as the procurement agent. Detailed analysis of the tender documents eventually convinced them that all was fair and above board. In fact, more equipment (by value) came from Germany than other countries.

We decided to retain ownership. All equipment was painted white and bore the EU logo and number plates. The political agreement, signed by both mayors, specified that we retained the right to repossess the equipment and export it without obstruction. This was a precaution, but probably more theoretical than real.

We decided to appoint two existing firms (one east, one west) as managing agents, who would receive a fee based mainly on the profitability of their operation. Since builders were encouraged to operate commercially, they were to be charged an economic fee for equipment hire. The equipment was a donation to the city, but it was to be well maintained and also, of course, would need to be replaced in several years' time, after the EUAM had ceased to exist. This was a business operation with a built-in incentive to the management agent. But beyond that, profit would be returned by the agent to the city council.

Dick Mills was an astute business manager as well as an engineer, and he worked out the business plan in great detail, as well as training the firms and monitoring their performance. Dick and I drafted the agency agreement together. It was checked and approved by the EUAM Legal Adviser.

Before the equipment was delivered—in stages from mid-1995 to early 1996—we had to repair two factories as maintenance depots and garages. Leases were signed with the owners, including a rent-free period in recognition of the cost of repair. After that, the managing agent would pay an agreed rent which would be covered by the projected profit. Maintenance equipment was supplied and staff given technical training. A 'procedures manual' was written by Dick covering every aspect of operation, both financial and technical.

By late 1995, both businesses were operating well, and making a substantial profit. The efficiency of the construction industry was visibly improving. In early 1995, we began to discuss arrangements for handing over the ownership to a local body. This had been considered at the beginning, and the original agency agreement specifically provided for the EUAM to donate the equipment to a 'successor body', to whom its rights and obligations would be transferred. We decided to transfer our position as owner to the unified city council, which had been elected by that time. However, we provided that, should the council cease to exist, then the equipment garaged in the east would revert to the east municipality, and similarly, that in the west would revert to the west. I drafted a deed of gift and had it checked by EC lawyers in Brussels. This was signed by all parties at a pleasant ceremony in May 1996. The managing agents achieved a high level of utilisation and turned in a decent profit. This had been a relatively major source of income for the municipalities and would be, in future, for the city council.

The EU Training Centre

This project began life as a water company training centre. The two water companies had almost no trained and experienced engineers, and it was obvious that investment in physical repair would be wasted if there were no men able to operate the system. We therefore set aside a few rooms in the basement of my department's office. I had appointed Gilmore Hankey Kirke International (GHKI) as a consultant to produce an infrastructure repair strategy and to implement a leakage repair programme. Their staff in Mostar, Mick Green and Khatib Alam, enthusiastically took up the training task. The enthusiasm of the local people also was impressive. When learning to apply computer packages, they realised the need to improve their English, and so a demand for language training emerged. Subsequently, the importance of company management skills—particularly financial management—became clear, and so management courses were added to engineering, computing and languages.

It gave everyone great satisfaction to see Croats and Muslims working together so well, and I saw this as the forerunner of an integrated single water company. To share learning how to run the system is only a short step away from actually running it together.

The basement rooms were now no longer adequate, and we repaired a small building, known as the Dom Ribara—the former Fishermen's Club—as a training centre. At this point, many other organisations asked to talk about training. I had always wanted to cover the entire span of reconstruction training, but other sectors altogether—for example, the police—started to ask for training. The Chief of Staff, Sir Martin Garrod, then weighed in to support a much bigger initiative to cover a wide field. I think he could see the great political potential in the idea that both sides might be trained together.

Before the Dom Ribara repairs were completed, therefore, the EUAM began to repair a bigger building (at Onesukova b.b.). We appointed a Spanish training consultancy from Valencia and the University of York (Institute of Advanced Architectural Studies) to develop courses and organise material and equipment.

Then, shortly before the opening—planned for September 1995—disaster struck. The Muslim owner (a Vakuf trust in name, but led by the east side's Legal Officer) sent in private guards, seized and padlocked the building. He justified his action by obscure legal argument, but I suppose the motive was to seize an asset for exclusive Muslim use. Perhaps I am mistaken, but I could see no other agenda.

Six months of frustrating argument followed. How much time was wasted! The building, with its costly equipment, books and furniture, lay unused. The end of the EU mandate drew closer, and we had to decide how to end the affair cleanly before we departed. My local Muslim colleagues were utterly appalled, and advised us to send in our police. But that was not our style.

In the end, I wrote a paper which analysed the options, and recommended, however reluctantly, that we should hand over the assets to the east side. By this time, Mr Koschnick had resigned, and the Administrator was an amiable Spaniard, formerly a city mayor. He agreed, and I drafted a deed of gift to transfer the assets to the east side's university, which in this case really meant the Muslim municipality. This was signed shortly before the end of the mandate. It was a sad episode.

Building Materials Laboratory

Every city needs laboratory facilities to test building materials in order to control the quality of construction. On the east side, there was no adequate laboratory. A minor facility near the Mostar dam had been damaged during the destruction of the hydro-electric power station. The EUAM therefore repaired this building and provided the necessary scientific equipment. This project was managed by Dick Mills. It was owned and operated by the east side municipality, and will for many years enhance their ability to enforce sound standards of building construction.

Conclusion

This area of our work was hard-fought internally. I failed to create the comprehensive and integrated strategy at which I had initially aimed. But I think there were significant successes. I particularly regret our failure to upgrade the quantity and quality of local materials and component production. For example, the quality of joinery and roof tiles was bad and got no better during our presence in the city.

Chapter 11

Urban Infrastructure

The Overseas Development Administration, part of the British Foreign Office, and now known as the Department for International Development (DfID), had operated the so-called Emergency Engineering Unit in Bosnia since 1992. It already had two staff in Mostar when the EUAM was established: Denver Brown was working on water supply and Tom Connolly on power. They had done heroic work under fire to restore some vital services, although it was partial and unreliable. Denver left in December 1994 and Tom transferred to the EUAM and stayed for a further two years. They were a great help in getting us off to a flying start. Denver Brown had in part resolved the emergency in early 1994 by installing a generator and pump to take untreated water from the river to supply the east side distribution network, although the pressure was too low to reach higher ground or top floors.

Two other agencies were undertaking important projects when the EUAM was set up. Technisches Hilfswerk (THW) was attempting the repair of Studenac Well Field but had encountered serious practical problems, and project completion was long delayed. It was also repairing Mazoljiće Reservoir and subsequently also rebuilt a water main crossing of the river (near Lučki Bridge). The International Committee of the Red Cross (ICRC) was also supplying materials to allow repair of secondary distribution networks in the Cernica and Donja Mahala neighbourhoods as well as the Djikovina pumping station. However, labour was not paid, and action by the water companies was rather slow. It took six months of sustained effort by the EUAM to establish a complete and reliable supply.

The infrastructure companies were in a sad condition. Not only had their systems been balkanised into scarcely functional bits, but their skilled staff were mostly gone, their equipment and buildings had been destroyed and their income flow had dried up. The west water company director was well intentioned, but was a purely political appointment with no knowledge of engineering or business. The east director was a distinguished engineer, but he was a specialist in the design of high dams. However gifted he was, such a background was not an ideal preparation for managing an urban infrastructure company.

No one had taken an overview of the problem, preoccupied as they naturally were with emergency responses. I therefore appointed a British consultant team (GHKI and Kennedy Donkin) to review the condition of all systems and propose a two-year action plan based on my best guess at the total budget. They arrived in early October and took the very short space of two months to report. This report covered water, sanitation, power, solid waste and telecommunications. I stressed the need to consider not only physical repairs but also equipment, personnel and finance, with the aim of creating so far as possible a sustainable operation before the end of our mandate.

The brief encompassed all such infrastructure, because we wanted a coordinated approach. It soon emerged, however, that the different EU member states demanded a slice of the action. In the ensuing carve-up, electricity was transferred to the Economy Department, telecommunications to the Department of Cultural Life, Youth and Sports and solid waste to the City Administration Department. I was left with responsibility for water and sewerage, and, apart from some failed attempts at coordination, I settled down to focus on this. The following therefore concerns itself mainly with water, although equally sound work was done in the other sectors and l hope that the story of that can be recorded in due course.

Implementation

By January 1996, l had recruited two Water Project Managers. Drazen Milićić was a young and gifted engineer from Croatia. He was joined by Zoran Milašinović, who had been a senior man in the Sarajevo water company and a Professor of Engineering at the university there. They were led by Jorge Ditzel Neumann, who was sent by the Spanish Government as my deputy. Valuable back-up was provided by the consultants who were intermittently present until June 1996.

In September 1994 we established a water committee with the directors and staff of the two water companies, and representatives of THW, ICRC and others. It met every week for two years and directed all work. After Jorge arrived in January, I transferred the chairmanship to him.

Most contracts were executed as direct works by the water companies. In major cases, we tendered competitively, but in many cases, the water company won. The largest contracts, including the Rades High Zone Supply Project, were all won by private companies, however.

I am not generally in favour of direct works by municipal companies, but in 1994 there was literally no choice. By early 1995, the war around Mostar subsided, and other options emerged. The water companies owned the system, of course, and were responsible for operating it: their acceptance of works was therefore necessary. They put me under pressure to employ them for all works to their system. The merit of this was that it would generally enhance their capability for the future, but lack of competition would open the way for overcharging and complacency. Before the war, they had done all the work on their own system themselves, and others had never gained the relevant experience.

I felt it was wise to avoid too strong a challenge, since I needed to build a good relationship for broader reasons. I did insist, however, that precise designs and bills of quantities be prepared, and in cases where no competitive tendering occurred, we checked their cost rates and calculations carefully, and monitored the timesheets of their workers. Prior to January 1995, however, I had no staff, and I am sure that overcharging occurred. Because of this, the early pressure to save on EUAM staff costs led to a greater loss.

The Strategic Plan

The consultants' report contained a good summary of the inherited system and the damage it had sustained. They reviewed the water companies' urgent proposals and mostly recommended their acceptance. They discussed a total strategy with the water companies and put forward a commonly agreed programme. To this there was one major subsequent addition, namely the Rades High Zone Supply Project, which was not damage repair but rather a wholly new scheme, accepted by Mr Koschnick for political reasons.

There were ultimately 58 water contracts and 12 sewerage projects at a total cost of DM20.06 million. They fell into seven broad categories:

- repair of sources (such as wells, pumps, and reservoirs) and primary networks;
- repair of secondary networks in key inner city areas;
- leakage detection and repair;
- repair of damaged sewers and cleaning or maintenance;
- repair of company offices and workshops and supply of maintenance equipment, vehicles, spare parts etc.;
- miscellaneous items, such as electricity supply, chlorination equipment, remote control systems, fortification, etc.; and
- measures to re-establish the viability of the water companies, such as training and cost-recovery measures (including tariff-fixing, metering, and computer systems for business management, billing and collection etc.).

The rest of this chapter discusses key aspects of these seven areas. Data on the seventy contracts are given in Appendix One.

Sources and Primary Networks

All significant pre-war sources were on the west side, so that the Croats could have shut off water for the east, once it was repaired. It is only fair to say that the Croat water company showed no such hostile intention, and indeed, they cooperated closely with their Muslim colleagues as well as the EUAM. But the simple possibility was a sword of Damocles: I shall return to this issue later.

The repair of the Studenac Wellfield, north of the city, was completed by April 1995. We were very worried that the asbestos main from Studenac to the city, entering it on the west side, had been fractured by high levels of military activity, particularly as a result of tanks crossing it. To replace fractured pipes could have taken many months, during which the city would have been without water. This was an explosive grass-roots political issue and a test of our effectiveness. We put the main under medium pressure and tested for leaks. Happily, there were none.

The EUAM also constructed a new main from Studenac, crossing the river at Mostar Dam and entering the city on the east side. In future, new wells on the east side, north of the city, could have been connected to this main, thus supplying water to the east side even if Studenac wells were closed. Additionally we constructed two new wells within the city on the east side, feeding directly into the existing distribution network. These measures laid the basis for an independent supply to the east side. The cards were thus dealt more fairly. Neither I nor others identified the political dimension to this: it was never discussed in those terms. The EUAM aim was to create a single water company operating an integrated system. But this would never happen if one side had all the sources. You can only get real cooperation between secure partners.

We also 'sweetened' the Croat side by building a new reservoir, pumping station electricity supply and primary mains for the Rades High Zone, which would supply water to the outer suburbs of Cim, Ilići and Vihovći. This area was the heartland of Croat extremists, and they had never had a mains supply before. This was a controversial decision. The cost was high and it was not war damage repair. However, the Croat mayor Brajković made a special appeal to Mr Koschnick who saw it as a political *quid pro quo* to buy political cooperation. In that sense, it did not work.

Secondary Networks

The EUAM set up a contract to rehabilitate the secondary distribution network in the entire central area of the east side. We also agreed to pay labour costs for work in those neighbourhoods (Luka, Donja Mahala and Cernica) for which THW and ICRC had supplied materials. This was a controversial decision, but I came to the view that the work would not otherwise proceed in a timely manner. We therefore set up proper contracts which allowed us to force the water companies to prepare proper documents, including designs and quantities, and gave us a basis for supervision. Remuneration allowed the companies to recruit competent manpower and set up a better management system. Without this, I suspect the donated materials would still be gathering dust in the warehouse.

Leak Detection and Repair

Before the war, 50 per cent of Mostar's water was unaccounted for and probably almost all of this was due to leakage. After the war, indications were that this had risen to 70 per cent. Obviously there was no hope for cost-recovery and financial sustainability if leakage was so great. There was no shortage of water at source, but the cost rate of production was high relative to the cost of stopping leakage.

I asked the consultants Khatib Alam and Mick Green to stay on in order to set up a continuous programme of leak detection and repair. Equipment was procured, and the water companies hired men to form a team dedicated to this task. Khatib and Mick undertook to train and supervise them. However, leak detection is a long, slow job (which should, of course, never stop). The EUAM mandate was short, and the EC refused to contemplate long-term support beyond July 1996. Nevertheless, good progress was made. First actions were to cut off water supply in war-damaged buildings which was flooding out into basements, squandering large amounts of this precious resource.

Sewerage

We purchased sewer-cleaning vehicles from Germany and set up several cleaning and repair contracts, focusing particularly on fractured connections from inhabited buildings which were flooding basements.

Sewerage pre-war had discharged into the river at many points, and a proposal had been made at that time to construct interceptor sewers along both banks leading to a treatment plant south of the city. The cost was estimated at DM90 million. It was obvious that the EUAM could not meaningfully fund even a part of this. However, we employed the Water Technology Institute of Sarajevo to prepare a consultancy report with the intention that it be presented to the World Bank for a long-term loan. More we would not do. This raised the issue of the unification of the water companies, since the Bank indicated that they were unwilling to handle the matter otherwise. I return to this general unification issue later.

Water Company Operation and Finance

As one of the EUAM's first acts, we set up contracts to repair the water company offices and workshops in Ricina Street, which had been on the front line. We also repaired old buildings on Tito Street (Mali Logor) to provide the east side with temporary accommodation. We procured equipment, including lorries and excavators, as well as spare parts and materials, such as chlorine. We fortified key points to withstand bombardment. We also set up a training scheme, as described in Chapter 10.

None of this touched the basic problem which all such companies face, namely how to create an income flow, and how to manage expenditure in the context of a viable business plan. As soon as I arrived in Mostar, I said that we must not use our money like opium, breeding dependency (and later withdrawal shock), but rather as a benign drug to help the patient recover and sustain autonomy.

In October 1994 I asked the consultants to address this question generally in their strategy study, which they did. My view (which is the usual wisdom) was that the capital investment programme should be formulated in the light of a level of operation which could be brought to a sustainable state within a target time period. I proposed to follow the strategic plan with a business plan in which capital investment—beyond the purely humanitarian phase—would be part of the strategy for continuing operation. Specifically, I asked the consultants to consider whether a subsidy, perhaps consumer-based rather than producer-based, tapering over time, was needed in order to allow the company to build up an effective user charging mechanism.

This was blocked by the Director of Finance and Taxes and led to a long-running argument. At that early stage, he appeared to have no interest in the creation of sustainable finance, and nor indeed did other EUAM colleagues. I foolishly underestimated this opposition, and set up the necessary consultancy contract. I was forced to curtail this in mid-1995, two weeks after my consultants had started work. But within three months the sky was dark with chickens coming home to roost. The water company in the west came to the point of breakdown. Its staff could not be paid, and they left for other work. It could not pay its bills, and supplies, notably electricity, were curtailed. They then asked the east side to pay for the water which they were receiving free of charge. The east side resisted. They were not, at that point, self-sufficient, and a major east-west political conflict grew. They agreed only on one point—the EUAM was to blame.

My water staff then did excellent work on financial diplomacy between east and west. We installed bulk flow meters at all east-west connections, analysed the company accounts and negotiated an agreement on the charge per litre as well as the terms of payment. But, of course, the basic problem of negligible income flow remained.

Sir Martin Garrod had stood aside from the argument until then but he now weighed in with characteristic insight and decisiveness. We therefore restarted the work to prepare a business plan. Both companies cooperated fully, and contributed to the final result, which they fully endorsed. It was completed in February 1996, shortly before the end of the EUAM. We had little time left, and more significantly, all the money was spent or irrevocably committed. We had done the first task last and missed the boat. However, we took some cheap, preparatory steps during autumn 1995, such as the purchase of meters to allow major customers to be charged. We also purchased hardware and software to allow billing, collection and accounting.

I was in touch with the Sarajevo office of the World Bank, and they showed great interest in our business plan. Our consultants held several meetings with their opposite numbers at the Bank, and the Bank agreed in principle to finance it provided that both companies agreed to abide by the envisaged arrangements. The two companies agreed and said they were happy to unify their technical and financial management according to the proposals. Given the opportunity the Bank offered them, this was not altogether surprising.

Conclusion

I had no cause to complain about the conduct of the water companies. During the first meetings, there was a good deal of hostility. This was understandable—particularly from the east side Director Professor Dr Mehmet Sarić, who in the darkest days had undertaken running repairs (and even built a suspension bridge over the river, mostly from scavenged materials) under sniper fire. But soon an excellent spirit emerged. Sarić and his Croat colleague, Mario Mikulić, actually became friends and would appear on all social occasions together, rather like twins, and when called upon to make a speech, always did a harmonious double act. My staff and I came to like and respect them both and I am sure the feeling was reciprocal. Mikulić was no engineer; in any case, he was a nationalist and highly politicised. But I thought he was a decent and straightforward man. The EUAM missed the chance to build solid political progress on the base of the potential for unification in the water industry. With reason, few things are more political than water, but even the hardliners who hemmed Mikulić in said to me in 1994/95 that water was a common resource, and that it could only be managed as a single system.

Chapter 12

Conclusions

The first purpose of this book has been to record what the EUAM was, what it did and how it did it. The second purpose was to draw some lessons from its successes and its failures. Various lessons have been suggested in earlier chapters but, by way of a conclusion, four especially fundamental points will now be explored. These are as follows:

- the need to enhance the technical and managerial capabilities of the European Commission in relation to the type of mission it undertook in Bosnia;
- the importance of creating sustainable institutions for urban management and finance;
- the need to emphasise 'bottom-up' pragmatic/technical measures as well as 'top-down' idealistic/political measures in pursuing the goals of political stabilisation; and
- the importance of grasping the psychological and cultural perspective of the local parties and the need to base tactics upon the possibilities inherent in that, rather than upon the ideals or preconceptions of Europe (given that the power or will to force the issue was lacking).

These points obviously overlap and interlock, and that is reflected in the discussion.

The Commission's Role

When the EU set up its Mostar project, it took some excellent decisions. It created a self-sufficient and integrated task force permanently on the ground. This was given a strong leader, and the EU delegated all matters of importance, including contractual and financial decisions. In Chapter 3, I described this as the 'Mostar model'. It had never been done before by Brussels and has not been repeated since. There were defects, which are reviewed below, but the Mostar principles should be used again because (a) the defects can be rectified easily and (b) the alternative— namely a Commission delegation—has not succeeded in Bosnia as a whole and is unlikely to do so in similar situations elsewhere. These two reasons are considered in turn.

First, the defects are considered together with their means of correction. There was little serious advance planning and no continuous monitoring/guidance system in technical respects. This was due to the six-monthly rotation of the EU Presidency and the absence of technical or project management experts in the permanent staff of the Commission. A permanent 'Task Force Steering Unit', staffed by experts, could have been established in Brussels. A Steering Unit would have overcome the inability of a dispersed and complex bureaucracy to respond to urgent questions which Mostar sent to Brussels and to capitals. This inability was noticed by the Court of Auditors.

Also, it could, for instance, have pre-planned manpower resources and directed recruitment of expatriates in a professional way. It could have guided the creation of an implementation system, such as methods of financial control, contract forms, tendering rules etc., at the beginning, avoiding the vacuum which arose in 1994 and was not fully resolved for six months.

Another issue was inappropriate time horizons and lack of continuity of vision (described and also discussed in Chapter 3). The habit of refusing to think ahead, and the inability to take timely decisions, allied to a preference for grandiose aims, was counter-productive. It suggested a lack of seriousness—or, at least, of realism. The presence of experienced experts in the original planning group would have led to a more sensitive and realistic phasing. A medium-term technical assistance programme would have allowed us to consolidate the gains for the longer term and reap the returns on the investment already made.

In short, the defects in the EUAM could have been resolved by quite normal, practical and inexpensive means. But the second point is that the only alternative to such a task force would have been a delegation of the Commission. It is important to pause to consider this point.

If you want to lift a tree, you need an elephant, but to fly or catch a rabbit you need a falcon. It would be foolish to criticise the falcon or the elephant. They are both fine in their way, and one is not wishing in this sense to criticise the Commission. It is nonetheless an elephant whereas some tasks require a falcon. The EU recognised this in the case of Mostar, and much of the credit for that should go to my old friend and sparring partner, Klaus von Helldorff, a Commission official who became the EUAM Director of Finance and Taxes.

When, in 1995, the Commission wanted to achieve in Bosnia as a whole what the Union had done so well in Mostar, it set up a delegation in Sarajevo. To be blunt, it was a failure (at least until the time of writing). I saw something of its operation, because in 1996 I was asked to take over the management of some urgent projects outside Mostar. I was stunned by what I saw. What could be decided formally in one day in Mostar took the Commission six to nine months to decide. And the quality of the decisions was inferior: the Parliament Building is a case in point.

So far as I could see, this arose from five factors. First, there were no technical experts or professional project managers on the permanent staff in Brussels or Sarajevo. One was therefore communicating with people who, while they may have been good public officials, knew nothing of technical matters or of project management processes. Second, practically nothing was delegated from the centre. Third, the responsibility for these decisions was so widely dispersed within the remote Brussels machine that no individual could be readily found to carry the burden. Fourth, the culture was focused on procedure and not on results. In other words, the means had been elevated into pseudo-ends, with the result that real ends could not be treated as urgent and time lost its meaning. Fifth, the procedures, which are merely tools, were not fashioned to create the product desired in the time available.

This led to considerable frustration and alienation which contrasted with the 'can do' optimism and solidarity of the Mostar team. It is important to add that this was not due to the failure of individuals but rather to the systemic inappropriateness of the machine itself relative to the demands of the particular type of task. It was unfair that some individuals on the EC staff took the blame in the scramble of recrimination. Rapid and effective action by large agencies in Bosnia is perfectly feasible, as the World Bank, the ODA and THW clearly demonstrated.

The EC bureaucratic elephant is, I suppose, competent to move a great weight slowly. But for rapid results in complex, dynamic contexts, it is not really appropriate. The 'Mostar model' is a practical and realistic alternative, proven in practice. The Commission would be foolish indeed if, in a defensive spirit, it refused to develop and apply it in appropriate future cases. To refuse any surrender of central power is to lose it altogether when events spin out of your control. More falcons please, but trained to return to the falconer's wrist when the job is done!

Repair of Systems or Repair of Objects?

Sometimes it seemed as if the EUAM strategy was media-driven. A repaired object can be videoed for television and there is a precise occasion for celebration and congratulation. A process of institutional upgrading cannot be photographed. Its completion is not an event in time, and it cannot so easily be dramatised and quantified for use in a propaganda war. One can understand and sympathise with the politicians' insatiable demand for objects and events, but it is nonetheless ultimately counter-productive.

Chapters 3 and 11 described the argument for the creation of sustainable processes for the management and finance of urban systems. It was suggested that this is more significant than the repair of objects *per se*, which should be directed by and achieved through the repair of local systems. In the wider world, development professionals learnt this lesson long ago, when they observed how much money was wasted on rusting relics which had not been sustained by local institutions after the aid project had ended.

In particular, sustainable finance is the key. The EUAM, in the persons of Mr Koschnick and Mr Klaus von Helldorff, quite openly refused to contemplate the creation of public finances able to outlast the EUAM mandate (and that is a matter for the record). In arguing that this was a practical and political impossibility, von

Helldorff may have been both wise and right. But nevertheless, it was obviously implied as a duty by the Memorandum of Understanding. It led to an argument between Klaus and myself, but due to his good humour and expansive personality, we remained good friends! If one supposes that Klaus was even half right in this matter, then that is a critical issue to be pondered by future policy-makers in Brussels.

In early 1997, around the time of my departure, Boro Puljić, who was my Croat Co-Director, wrote an interesting letter to me. It reflected critically, but constructively, upon the legacy of the EUAM. I will quote from it extracts which concern these issues. Perhaps he overstates or oversimplifies the argument, but his remarks contain some important truths, to which the European Commission should pay attention.

> Instead of donating us fishing rods and teaching us how to catch fish, we were constantly being donated the ready-caught fish.

> For the EUAM it was necessary in a humanitarian emergency to start the reconstruction process so as to create the minimum of living conditions in the city but at the same time it was a chance to use physical reconstruction as a means of creating processes of general development. There was also a chance to correct a lot of irregularities in the earlier functioning of the city. Until then the city had functioned as an organised socialist state, and under the EU there was a chance for the system to switch to market conditions.

> With good organisation and planning, sustainable local economic processes could have been started with the money that had flowed in. Instead of such a meaningful approach, the EU just decided to reconstruct all the schools, then all the kindergartens, then the bridges, social institutions, etc. No optimal level of investments was determined, nor was the remaining money invested in creating the conditions for labour by the surplus of which the public facilities could have been maintained or new ones constructed after the EU had departed. So today we have beautiful school buildings, but there are no funds to paint them or to buy the school children a new blackboard.

> So the reconstruction process during the stay of the EUAM has never been made meaningful or planned in order to give the citizens a long-term functional city system that would make possible the collection of revenue and its spending for the long term reconstruction of the destroyed fabric and maintenance of the city services as well as for the construction of further infrastructure.

> Through a planned approach, Mostar could have become a part of a system of well organised European cities. Upon the departure of the EUAM an inner financial reserve and a system should have been left behind which would have allowed the reconstruction process to proceed under its own steam.

This means that the reconstruction process under the aegis of the EUAM should have been a prime-mover of future development. The money brought by the EUAM and other humanitarian organisations (more than DM300 million) could have been an initial means. In an optimal and market-oriented city system created in this way, *the reconstruction process could also have become a medium for an easier development of political processes.*

The building engineers used to say that in Mostar it is the buildings that are being reconstructed, not the life in the city.

The EUAM should not have become a humanitarian organisation. Instead it should have invested the money in creating new opportunities for employment (not just as donations but to get that money back into the process through banks) and by developing a market economy. This would have allowed the city to build its own infrastructure and public utilities, as well as health, education and similar facilities.

At the same time, only minimal funds should have been invested in the facilities of social superstructure—sufficient only to allow the functioning of health, education and other systems at a level just adequate to sustain existence. Instead of becoming a European experiment and discovery, Mostar has become a European Casablanca and El Dorado.

Top-Down Versus Bottom-Up

There was a 'top-down' process of seeking resolution of high-level political questions before proceeding (in a linear fashion) to construct the institutional arrangements for urban management. By 'bottom-up' is meant the reverse tactical process of building a non-controversial institutional machine first, and proceeding by stages towards a resolution of the broader political questions. It often seems that top-down tactics appeal to the mind of the politician and the diplomat, whereas the bottom-up tactics appeal to the mind of the technician.

This is, of course, a false dichotomy between idealism and pragmatism, and in reality both should be pursued, with a continuous process of feedback and adjustment in order to synthesise a coherent and practical strategy. But this is a dynamic model, not a static one. It requires an experimental attitude and a willingness to rapidly reformulate objectives and methods. To put it another way, one must fight in depth and move at speed rather than dig into fixed trenches.

In Mostar we worked both from the top down and the bottom up, but the two strands of work were not altogether synthesised, and (in my opinion) the potential bottom-up contribution to political progress was not sufficiently realised. The political work stream focused upon reaching global agreement on principles to do with freedom of movement, integration of the police force, elections to a single city council and so on. The urban management machine was regarded as a technical detail, which could be readily resolved by others after the global principles had been agreed between the parties. It was not really seen to be a task for the EUAM at all. But the local parties felt insecure and acted with intransigence on global political matters. The grand plan of the EU induced panic, and negotiations were mostly deadlocked, with each side refusing to compromise. Political progress was painfully slow. Meanwhile, the technicians made better progress at more humble tasks. We established a joint urban planning unit and a joint water company training centre. We almost established a joint construction equipment pool. Technical committees were integrated and the atmosphere was warm and cooperative. The reason for this was surely that such technical cooperation was not perceived as threatening, and people were happy to proceed step by step to create a better life. Nonetheless, the political deadlock clouded the horizon and bottom-up improvements did not proceed as well as I had envisaged.

If the vision of the political officers had been pursued a little more flexibly or imaginatively, the local leaders would have panicked less. In these circumstances, and working step by step from the bottom up, I think we could have created competent and properly functioning urban management institutions, shared, if not fully integrated. I felt that there was a greater need for sustainable institutions of technical and financial administration and that they were more conducive to political stabilisation in the real world than were the visions of the diplomats. After all, you build a house from the ground up, and an oak grows from an acorn.

I found, moreover, that the locals were eager to experiment in this step-by-step, practical way. I think we could have pushed back the political boundaries of the possible quite some distance, because the grand political vision would not have been at stake at any particular point. Fears on that plane would not have blocked useful technical and administrative improvements. After all, everyone welcomes such improvement if the values they hold are not threatened. Such step-by-step change ultimately drives grand political change, rather than the other way round.

But the EUAM was very much dominated by diplomats, politicians, lawyers and so on. In fact, I was the only development expert on the senior expatriate staff. I felt that I was seen as a pure 'bricks and mortar' man, whereas development expertise does encompass all matters relevant to the operation of cities, including public finance, administration, infrastructure management, economic development, cultural change, and so on. Incidentally, I felt I had more in common with our soldiers than with our politicians and diplomats. Soldiers are practical results-oriented planners and managers.

The lessons here, in my own opinion, are first to give a somewhat stronger role to development expertise so that the perspective of diplomats and lawyers is tempered, and second, to achieve better feedback between these two perspectives by corporate committee work and brainstorming. In the EUAM, there was little such activity, as noted in Chapter 3, and each stream of work was pursued somewhat in isolation, not only practically but also intellectually.

Navigating the Maze

Finally, I would like to discuss the importance of grasping the psychological and cultural perspective of the local parties, conducting dialogue in the language of the adversaries' world-view, and negotiating towards a deal which makes sufficient sense in the framework of *their* calculus. The local parties often said that the EU did not understand them at all, and that our objectives were utopian. I am afraid that they were not entirely wrong. If so, that could be the main reason why the political work was not very successful—at least during the mandate period.

One option in theory would have been to seize the country; remove tainted leaders and replace them with good ones; prosecute malefactors; restructure institutions so as to create a free press, independent judiciary, parliamentary democracy and market economy; and radically re-educate the people. We did not do this, and so were obliged to negotiate with an existing elite, from whose hands we would not wrest the real levers of power. Indeed, parts of that elite we would not even speak to for moral or political reasons.

And yet we pursued an immensely ambitious agenda in an inflexible way. Herein lies the contradiction—that our politicians and diplomats willed the ends, but did not will the means. But if the means are given, then the ends must always be commensurate, since otherwise you will bang your head on a brick wall. That is what happened. 'Es muss sein, es muss sein' (it must be, it must be), shouted Klaus Kinkel in impotent rage.

The EU wanted everyone to be returned to their original homes; universal freedom of movement; elimination of the Croat proto-state ('Herceg-Bosna'); and the unification of civil government, including the police. The local agenda seemed to be about ethnic identity, group territory, viability in economic (and perhaps military) terms, and political and cultural hegemony.

Parts of the current Bosnian elite lives in an authentic pre-modern moral universe—Aquinas' notion of *pietas*; that is, the defence of family and national honour under the leadership of a 'great soul'. This idea died for us in Flanders, but for many Bosnians it still lives and seems to them to justify morally what in our eyes may be crimes.

I found that the book *On Aggression*, by the biologist Konrad Lorenz, threw much light on Bosnia for me. The need for group allegiance as the means to forge a secure personal identity and the need to expel non-members in order to maintain an integrated sense of self; the relationship of identity to territory, and the need to mark boundaries; the instinctively violent response to territorial invasion, and so on—all these ideas have obvious resonance. Furthermore, religion—particularly Christianity—has been mobilised in order to sanctify this (to us) primitive conduct. The Titoist claims about the relationship between Cardinal Aloysius Stepinac and the Pavelic regime seemed to me more believable after talking to the holy fathers in Mostar Monastery!

So I think that this moral universe has its own tenacious logic, and it would not be so strange to Homer, Shakespeare, Machiavelli, Carlyle, Fichte or indeed to most people living before the present century. The EU did not argue with reference to the logical frame of their adversaries' belief system, and so it seemed to be a dialogue of the deaf.

Could the agendas of the EU and the locals have been synthesised? The best chance would have arisen from a creative, imaginative response by the EU using the logic of the locals to address *not* our preconceived targets, but rather the common-sense basics emerging organically from really pragmatic discussion. My own view, incidentally, favoured settlement of displaced persons in majority territory (with compensation) plus territorial hegemony through multi-tier government of the Belgian type. Surely it is better to have a safe, decent house in a new area *now*, than to have your old house in an unsafe area some time in the future (or never). In the long run, we are all dead, as Keynes said. Making normal, everyday, people feel safe will allow authentic, unforced cooperation to begin and to flourish, and will also isolate extremists and allow moderates gradually to take over. Perhaps developmental psychology can be applied to societies as well as individuals. Piaget pointed out that humans progress through developmental stages, and that if parents force the speed of change, then the child gets stuck at an uncompleted stage, even though they continue to age chronologically. Is it not also true for societies? Cultural change has its own natural, organically determined speed, which can be manipulated like a plant, but not disregarded. Pulling on a plant does not make it grow faster.

It was difficult for technicians like me to get a handle on the political project. It seemed to be too vague and too utopian in its formulation to permit us to contribute effectively. If, however, practical, concrete political proposals had been thrashed out early on, then the technical programmes could have been formulated and harnessed to give reality to them. Then one could probably have shown how specific technical work had contributed to the realisation of specific political programmes, whereas, in reality, such links were scarcely made. The technical work was largely self-directed, and the political spin-offs which did in fact arise were not promoted (or even seized upon) by political and diplomatic officers.

The MOU was a fine document, but the use subsequently made of it had two defects—it was both inflexible and abstract. The MOU became a substitute for creative thought about strategic alternatives, and also the nitty-gritty questions of 'how'. It was repeated like a mantra, and negotiations were fought from fixed trenches. I use the phrase 'navigating the maze' to indicate a process of discovery and revision in moving towards an unknown destination, but also to hint at the need to uncover the world-view of the locals, which seems maze-like nonsense at first. But it has its own natural logic, which yields the key to the maze and allows us to emerge on to clear ground before night falls.

All this is, of course, the opinion of an amateur with little experience or knowledge of politics. Perhaps I am seriously wide of the mark, and my observations will be (and should be) treated with due scepticism. Also, of course, my points represent a snapshot at one time, and since then, Sir Martin Garrod has worked as the head of the regional office of the High Representative. I gather that the situation in the city continues to improve and, of course, the EUAM is itself now part of history. The city council is slowly getting stronger, and new, moderate politicians are taking over. Sir Martin is a patient, but persistent professional, so that one may feel cautiously optimistic about the long term result.

Look, the Land is Bright!

At a low point, I gave Sir Martin a copy of Arthur Hugh Clough's famous poem which seemed to sum up our feelings rather well.

> Say *not* the struggle naught availeth;
> The labour and the wounds are vain;
> The enemy faints not, nor faileth;
> As things have been, so things remain.

> If hopes were dupes, fears may be liars;
> It may be, in yon smoke concealed,
> Your comrades chase e'en now the fliers,
> And, but for you, possess the field.

> For while the tired waves, vainly breaking,
> Seem *here* no painful inch to gain,
> Far back through creeks and inlets making
> Comes silent flooding in, the main.

> And not by eastern windows only,
> When daylight comes, comes in the light.
> In front the sun climbs slow, how slowly,
> But westward, look, the land is bright!

Appendix 1

Project Schedules

Note: Other EUAM projects in the fields of telecommunications, education and culture, electricity and bridge building are not included here. The author was unable to obtain reasonably complete data at the time of writing (they had been the responsibility of other departments).

In due course, final accounts of expenditure will be published by the EU. The financial figures given here are not complete or final, and should be regarded as an interim statement only.

Table 1 *Light damage housing repair contracts*

Contract name		Contract value (DM)	Contractor	Execution period
1994 project for 2500 dwellings east				10/94–5/95
• Materials		3 750 000	THW	
• Labour		1 250 000	Zidar	
• Fees (survey)		230 000	Municipal agencies	
	TOTAL	5 230 000		
1994 project for 1000 dwellings west				10/94–5/95
• Materials		1 500 000	Slavonija Trgovina	
• Labour		250 000	Konstrucktor	
• Fees (survey)		92 000	Municipal agencies	
	TOTAL	1 842 000		
1995 project for 440 dwellings east				6/95–4/96
• Materials		880 000	THW	
• Labour		296 000	Various	
• Fees (survey)		15 984	Municipal agencies	
	TOTAL	1 176 984		
1995 project for 1100 dwellings west				6/95–5/96
• Materials		1 100 000	Slavonija Trgovina	
• Labour		275 000	Konstruktor	
• Fees (survey)		99 000	Municipal agencies	
	TOTAL	1 474 000		
1996 project for 301 dwellings east				5/96–11/96
• Materials		1 200 000	THW	
• Labour		600 000	Various	
• Fees (survey)		39 000	Municipal agencies	
	TOTAL	1 839 000		

Table 2 *Medium and heavy damage housing repair contracts*

	Contract name	Contract value (DM)	Contractor	Execution period
1	Luka 1	555 328	Gradnja Zenica	6/95–6/96
2	Brankovac	624 373	Gramos Mostar	6/95–4/96
3	Luka 2	412 044	Neimar Stolac	6/95–7/96
4	Carina, Zalik and Vrapćići	577 551	IGM Visoko	7/95–7/96
5	Donja Mahala	730 640	Zvijezda Visoko	7/95–10/96
6	Cernica	194 091	Izgradnja Invest Zenica	8/95–6/96
7	Luka 1 and 2	602 158	Mali Komerc	12/95–12/96
8	D. Mahala and Cernica	613 772	Zvijezda Visoko	12/95–12/96
9	Brankovac and Carina	458 641	Zening, Zenica	12/95–12/96
10	Materials Only Package	534 000	THW	12/95–6/96
11	Potoci-Vojno 1, 2, 3	1 041 614	n.a.	n.a.
12	Vrapćići 1, 2, 3	2 159 699	n.a.	n.a.

Note: The Potoci-Vojno (west) and Vrapćići (east) contracts were in villages north of the city. Regrettably the author left Mostar without full data and has been unable to obtain it subsequently. N.a. denotes 'not available'.

Table 3 *Apartment block contracts*

	Contract name	Contract value (DM)	Contractor	Execution period
1	Revija Building	1 265 205	Kemos, Mostar	5/95–5/96
2	Tito Street, No. 82	1 066 694	Kemos, Mostar	5/95–12/95
3	Šantića Street, No. 4	782 657	Izgradnja Invest Zenica	5/95–3/96
4	Bejrut Building	1 461 154	GP Bosna	5/95–4/96
5	Adema Buća Street 24/26	355 660	SZR Cernica	4/96–8/96
6	Soliter Tower, Zalik	869 496	Izgradnja Invest Zenica	4/96–10/96
7	Kamena Building	709 714	Tuca Produkt	4/96–9/96
8	Adema Buća Street, 17	611 505	SZR Cernica	10/95–6/96

Table 4 *Housing component repair contracts*

	Contract name	Contract value (DM)	Contractor	Execution period
1	Pumps in tower blocks	281 801	Elektrokovina	1/96–7/96
2	Lifts in tower blocks	518 288	Končar Zagreb	1/96–7/96
3	Flat roofs 1 west	107 469	Borak	4/96–7/96
4	Flat roofs 2 west	108 165	Bitas	4/96–7/96
5	Flat roofs 3 west	102 112	n.a.	4/96–6/96
6	Flat roofs 4 west	102 572	PUR	4/96–7/96
7	Pitched roofs 1 west	87 714	Vegrad	4/96–6/96
8	Pitched roofs 2 west	84 975	n.a.	4/96–6/96
9	Pitched roofs 3 west	86 595	Dzidic	4/96–6/96
10	Flat roofs east	488 385	Zidar	11/95–8/96
11	Pitched roofs east	463 765	Tehnograd Tuzla	11/95–6/96
12	Communal heating – west	482 976	Montprojekt	5/96–12/96
13	Communal heating – east	548 323	Montprojekt	7/96–12/96
14	Tekija (electrical, water and sanitation)	333 429	Instalater	4/95–6/96
15	Doors and windows	354 000	THW	10/95–6/96

Table 5 *Health and social services*

	Contract name	Contract value (DM)	Contractor	Execution period
1	Rehabilitation Centre	246 471.51	LS Company	8/95–1/96
2	Dom Zdravlja	3 547 145.00	Exportdrvo Zagreb	9/96–6/97
3	Institute of Hygiene	1 974 844.33	Unioninvest Sarajevo	8/95–4/96
4	Kruševo Clinic	110 212.93	Cubus	7/95–1/96
5	Zalik Clinic	366 255.00	Bosna Sarajevo	5/95–10/95
6	Blagaj Clinic	403 118.00	Zidar	5/95–7/96
7	South Camp General Hospital – Phase I	337 095.13	Rad Konjic, Tomas Co	7/95–10/95
8	Tekija Clinic	233 146.00	Zvijezda Visoko	9/95–5/96
9	South Camp General Hospital – Phase II	1 256 664.71	Zvijezda Visoko	9/95–6/96
10	Rudnik Clinic	161 389.63	Cubus	10/95–4/96
11	Buna Clinic	559 686.01	Cubus	4/96–1/97
12	Donja Mahala Clinic Phase I	404 806.05	LS Company	9/96–12/96
13	Donja Mahala Clinic Phase II	94 637.77	LS Company	9/96–12/96
14	South Camp Admin Offices	249 381.30	Zvijezda	5/96–10/96
15	South Camp General Hospital – Phase III	3 859 603.81	Unioninvest Sarajevo	4/96–6/97
16	Psychiatry South Camp	262 301.36	Zvijezda	1/96–6/96
17	Brankovac Paediatric Hospital – Phase I	1 756 129.35	Smelt Ljubljana	8/95–1/97
18	Brankovac Paediatric Hospital – Phase II	3 160 140.00	Smelt Ljubljana	11/95–3/97
19	Old People's Home, East	2 000 000.00	Dom Sarajevo	11/95–11/96
20	Centre for Social Work, East	457 753.47	Duraković Salko	11/95–7/96
21	Centre for Social Work (Temporary Offices)	12 000.00	LS Company	10/95–11/95

Table 6 *Miscellaneous building contracts*

	Contract name	Contract value (DM)	Contractor	Execution period
1	Hotel Mostar (police hostel)	916 804	Hercegovina Visokogradnja	7/95–6/96
2	Police Headquarters	810 000	Vranica Mostar	8/95–4/96
3	Police Station (East)	608 189	Vranica Sarajevo	9/95–4/96
4	Pensions & Social Insurance Building	27 560	Zidar	3/95–4/95
5	Fire Station	259 862	Grazit	4/96–6/96
6	Technical Agencies Office	425 538	Zidar	9/94–12/94
7	Higher Court	790 780	Vranica Mostar	3/96–11/96
8	Sutina Cemetery (mixed)	341 500	Zvijezda Visoko	6/95–8/95
9	Šoinovać Cemetery (catholic)	125 000	Parkovi	12/95–12/96
10	Public Works Depot	1 250 000	Tehnograd Tuzla	8/95–6/96
11	Public Works Depot landscaping	127 372	Hidrogradnja Sarajevo	5/96–7/96
12	Dom Ribara (Heritage Inst.)	107 793	Zidar	5/95–11/95
13	Cold Store	669 700	Hidrogradnja Sarajevo	8/95–10/95
14	Youth Centre	750 000	Vranica Mostar	6/95–11/95
15	Airport	862 824	Tipurić	4/96–3/97
16	Railway Station	1 478 685	Zidar, Mostar	1/96–6/96
17	Bus Station	300 000	Zidar, Mostar	4/96–6/96
18	Women's Cultural Centre ('Sumeja Building')	132 000	Zidar, Mostar	10/96–3/97
19	Mechanical Workshop, East	245 000	Zidar, Mostar	5/95–7/95
20	Mechanical Workshop, West	270 000	Hercegovina, Niskogradnja	5/95–7/95
21	EU Training Centre	735 000	Zening, Zenica	7/95–10/95
22	Hotel Bristol (hostel)	1 697 499	Kemos, Mostar	6/96–2/97
23	Old People's Shelter	60 065	Omer Čorda	12/94–1/95
24	Old People's Home (West)	703 439	Hercegovina Visokogradnja	12/94–1/95
25	Sanitary Landfill Site (Uborak)			4/96–3/97
	– earthworks	1 838 000	Kosmos, Mostar	
	– concrete	310 054	Tehnograd Tuzla	
	– drainage, ventilation	166 077	Unioninvest, Sarajevo	
	– metal work	61 234	Soko Imko	
	– membrane	532 801	Putevi Mostar	
	– electrical	153 040	Elektromontaža Tuzla	

Table 7 *List of construction equipment*

Item	Number
Flank tipper lorry (3 tons)	6
Rear tipper lorry (24 tons)	1
Flank tipper lorry (18 tons)	2
Rear tipper lorry (8 tons)	3
Lorry (6 tons)	1
Concrete mixer lorry (6 cubic metres)	4
Concrete pump lorry (80 cubic metres per hour)	1
Lorry-mounted crane (25 tons)	1
Mini-bus (20 persons)	2
Mini-bus (8 persons)	1
Bulldozer (D8/D9)	4
Loader (2.5 cu m/4 cu m)	4
Vibrating rollers	2
Dragline excavator (1.2 cu m)	1
Trench excavator	2
Compressor (7 cu cm per minute)	1
Bracket crane	5
Fork lift truck	2
Concrete vibrator (1.5 kw)	6
Rendering machine	1
Gypsum plastering machine	1
Mortar mixer (125 litre)	10
Scaffolding (2000 m^2 elevation)	–
Generator (15 kVA)	2

Note: This list excludes maintenance workshop equipment. The total cost was DM 8 396 675

Table 8 *Water contracts: works to sources and primary distribution*

	Contract name	Contract value (DM)	Contractor or supplier	Completion date
1	Musala Bridge Pipe (L)	25 800	UNPROFOR	10/94
2	Lučki Bridge Pipe (L)	28 880	Vodovod East	10/94
3	Mazoljiće Reservoir Rehabilitation – Civil (L)	50 250	Vodovod East	12/95
4	Mazoljiće Pump Station Rehabilitation	91 350	Vodovod East	6/95
5	Mazoliće Pump St Electrical and Mechanical Work	45 780	Pomak, Split	6/95
6	Water Intake, Carinski Bridge (L)	88 000	Vodovod East	3/95
7	Djikovina Pressurised Pipeline	115 820	Gradjevinar	3/95
8	Studenac Wellfield –			
	• pipeline repairs	8541	Gradjevinar	3/95
	• soil cleaning	25 000	Vodovod West	8/95
	• electrical supply	33 992	Comet, Ploce	10/95
	• fortification	20 000	UNPROFOR	6/95
	• sludge pump purchase and repair	12 990	Elektrokovina	2/96
	• generator repairs	29 400	Pomak, Split	2/96
	• electrical repairs	96 000	Pomak, Split	3/96
	• final works	176 363	Comet, Ploce	4/95
9	Main (500 mm) from Mostar Dam to City			
	• civil works	666 638	Vodovod East	1/97
	• pipes supply	1 155 792	AN Adria, Split	11/95
	• accessories supply	232 031	Palmir, Zagreb	12/96
10	Tube-Wells, East			
	• exploration	41 720	Geosonda, Zenica	6/95
	• well construction	169 000	Link, Zagreb	9/95
	• water stations	554 259	Vogel, Austria	12/95
	• connections, civil	92 870	Vodovod East	1/96
	• electrical works	30 000	Elektrodistribucija	1/96
11	Vrapćići Water Supply			
	• tube well construction	63 590	Link, Zagreb	2/96
	• pipes supply	56 410	Masa, Spain	2/96
	• water station	279 408	Vogel, Austria	7/96
	• materials	139 328	Hidropromet	10/96
	• civil works	99 000	Vodovod East	1/97

Note (L) denotes labour only, with materials supplied by others.

Table 8 *Water contracts works to sources and primary distribution*

	Contract name	Contract value (DM)	Contractor or supplier	Completion date
12	Concrete Plant Wells			
	• tube well construction	109 720	Link, Zagreb	1/96
	• pump and control gear	100 650	Vogel, Austria	3/96
13	Rades High Zone Project			
	• water materials supply I	936 552	Masa, Spain	8/96
	• water materials supply II	248 229	MIV, Varaždin	8/96
	• water materials supply III	75 000	Meteral, Sisak	6/96
	• electrical cables supply	80 000	EUAM	8/96
	• pump station equipment	133 484	Pomak, Split	1/97
	• reservoir construction	592 309	Niskogradnja Široki Brijeg	2/97
	• pump station construction	194 538	Hercegovina Niskogradnja	2/97
	• pressurised pipeline construction	168 984	Interinvest Mostar	2/97
	• distribution	2 277 123	Interinvest, Mostar	3/97
	• supervision and other fees	150 000	Vodovod and Water Institute	3/97
	• electricity transformer station construction	81 036	Končar, Split	11/96
	• laying power cable	62 999	Felix, Mostar	11/96
14	Fortification of Transformer	20 000	Vodovod East	3/95
15	Tube Wells in Posrt	38 000	Link Zagreb	11/95
16	Spare Parts for Water Stations	109 151	Vogel, Austria	8/96

Table 9 *Water contracts: secondary network*

	Contract name	Contract value (DM)	Contractor or supplier	Completion date
1	Cernica network rehabilitation (L)	74 150	Vodovod East	10/94
2	Luka network rehabilitation (L)	156 750	Vodovod East	3/96
3	Donja Mahala network rehabilitation (L)	97 040	Vodovod East	12/95
4	Central Zone network replacement	569 779	Vodovod East	10/96
5	Šantića Street network rehabilitation	99 000	Vodovod East	2/96

Note: (L) denotes labour only contract with materials donated by others.

Table 10 *Water contracts: leak detection and sewerage*

	Contract name	Contract value (DM)	Contractor or supplier	Completion date
	Leak detection			
1	Equipment	160 440	GTZ (Germany)	8/95
2	Materials, phase 1	225 000	TBS Croatia	8/95
3	Materials, phase 2	57 912	TBS Croatia	3/96
4	Labour contract	100 000	Vodovod East & West	3/96
	Sewerage			
5	Rehabilitation, East	118 202	Vodovod East	11/94
6	Maintenance, East	135 696	Vodovod East	11/94
7	Rehab./maintenance West	326 854	Vodovod West	3/95
8	Repair, Splitska Street	9 567	Vodovod West	10/94
9	Repair, Bulevar	5 034	Vodovod West	10/94
10	Rehabilitation, East, phase 2	400 000	Vodovod East	12/95
11	Rehabilitation, West, phase 2	200 000	Vodovod West	7/96
12	Rehabilitation, East, phase 3	150 000	Vodovod East	2/97
13	Consultancy design for complete sewerage system	233 000	Hidrotehnicki Institute, Sarajevo	7/96

Note: (L) denotes labour paid by EUAM and materials by others.

Table 11 *Water contracts: equipment and buildings*

	Contract name	Contract value (DM)	Contractor or supplier	Completion date
1	Office construction Mali Logor, East	129 600	Vodovod East	6/95
2	Office extension Mali Logor	81 000	Vodovod East	5/95
3	Laboratory, Studenac, West	94 240	THW	2/95
4	Workshop repair, Ricina Street, West	255 833	IPD Čitluk	11/95
5	Office repair, Ricina Street, West	395 207	IPD Čitluk	11/95
6	Garage construction Mali Logor, East	107 000	Vodovod East	4/95
7	Laboratory, East	197 500	Vodovod East	2/96
8	Metalwork shop, East	164 507	Vodovod East	5/95
9	Vehicle workshop, East	77 687	Vodovod East	3/96
10	Equipment, West			
	• furniture etc.	249 633	Dubint	4/95
	• equipment & tools	599 187	Mehanizacija	12/95
	• heating	209 412	Mehanizacija	5/95
	• phone system	20 376	Infosistem	4/95
	• electrical parts	83 250	Ellis Mostar	7/95
	• computers	144 786	Ecsat, Split	2/96
11	Furniture for Mali Logor	n.a.	Mediteks	6/95
12	Construction & maintenance equipment	719 835	Crown Agents (UK)	1/95
13	Construction & maintenance equipment (inc. flow meters)	1 000 000	GTZ (Germany)	4/96
14	Materials for Smrcenjaci	30 000	Brodomerkur Split	8/95
15	Chemicals for laboratories	52 000	Polopus, Zagreb	2/96
16	Chlorine	37 000	Polopus, Zagreb	2/96
17	Remote Control System I	95 300	Pomak, Split	12/95
18	Remote Control System II	74 700	Pomak Split	3/96
19	Billing System	95 000	Ecsat, Split	10/96

Appendix 2

Department Staff Listing

Note: Some of the staff listed below worked for the department for a long period and others for a shorter period. I sincerely apologise if I have inadvertently missed anyone's name off the list.

Deputy Director (Engineering)	Jorge Ditzel Neumann
Deputy Director (Urban Planning)	Francesco Aiello
Secretary to Director	Silvija Mikulić
Financial Officer	Meliha Denjo
Assistant Financial Officers	Dženana Dedić
	Selma Hadžiosmanović

INFRASTRUCTURE SECTION
Project Managers
Drazen Milićić
Zoran Milašinović
Khatib Alam (Consultant)
Mick Green (Consultant)

Secretary/Translators
Aner Kajtaz
Svjetlana Buhovać

CONSTRUCTION INDUSTRY SECTION
Project Managers
Richard Mills (Consultant)
Slaven Martinović

Secretary/Translator
Snjezana Damjanović

DEMOLITION AND RECYCLING SECTION
Project Managers
Niels Strufe (Consultant)
Martin Petersen (Consultant)
Simon Mitgaard Fogt (Consultant)

Secretary/Translator
Aida Kurtović
Marija Šilić

PLANNING SECTION
Project Managers
Marica Raspudić
Pero Marijanović

Secretary/Translator
Validan Puljić

BUILDINGS SECTION
Project Managers (Housing)
Hasan Čemalović

Secretary/Translators
Mirela Alikalfić

Alma Papić
Vladimir Petrović
Ozrenko Gačić
Leif Åmli

Mirna Picuga
Velibor Sudar
Danijela Pehar
Ivica Nikić
Nikola Pinjuh

Project Managers (Miscellaneous)
Abdurezak Abduzaimović
Dženana Maglajlić-Bijedić
Project Manager (Mechanical Engineering)
Zijo Kreso

HEALTH BUILDINGS SECTION
Note: This had been part of the Department of Health and Social Services, but transferred to the Department of Reconstruction in July 1996.

Project Managers
Jelica Rašeta-Jurišić
Zvonimir Petričević
Mevludin Zečević

Secretary/Translators
Jesenka Falak
Amira Ramić
Dražena Madzar

EDUCATION BUILDINGS SECTION
Note: This had been part of the Department of Education, but transferred to the Department of Reconstruction in July 1996.

Project Managers
Gerard Kuiper
Miro Mihić
Andreas Seebacher

Secretary/Translators
Dijana Kuzman
Tea Beaman

Bibliography

Note: This bibliography includes only items produced for or by (or otherwise relating to) the EUAM. Other works are not included. The list is highly selective, in the interests of brevity. The documents are now archived in Brussels and subject to certain rules of confidentiality. The list is divided into technical studies, legal documents and internal papers. The last two lists are in date order.

Technical Studies

Crown Agents, 'Study into the Construction Industry in Mostar', April 1995.

Crown Agents, 'EUAM Plant Hire Agency—Procedures Manual', 1995.

Demex Consulting Engineers A/S and Rambøll Hanneman Højlund A/S, 'Demolition & Building Waste Management System', 19 May 1995.

Demex Consulting Engineers A/S and Rambøll Hanneman & Højlund A/S, 'Single Demolition Contract—Final Report', 1996.

Deutsche Gesellschaft für Technische Zusammenarbeit (GTZ), 'Survey of War Damage in Mostar, Volumes One and Two—Survey. Volume Three—Maps', 1995.

GHKI (Gilmore Hankey Kirke International) in association with Kennedy & Donkin, 'Infrastructure Strategy & Investment Programme for Mostar: Final Report', December 1994.

GHKI, 'Recommendations on EUAM Support to the Water Supply & Distribution Industry in Mostar', 21 April 1995.

GHKI, 'Business Plan for the Water Industry in Mostar', 1996.

Saevfors Consulting, 'Population Survey for Mostar', 1995.

Legal Documents

Memorandum of Understanding on the European Union Administration of Mostar, 1994.

Decree on Demolition of Building Structures, EUAM, 1995.

Decree on Tenant's Rights, EUAM, 1995.

Decree on Fiduciary Management of Building Structures, EUAM, 1995.

Dayton Agreement on Implementing the Federation of Bosnia & Herzegovina of 10

November 1995: Annexe—Agreed Principles for the Interim Statute for the City of Mostar.

Official Gazette of the City of Mostar (20 February 1996), 'Interim Statute of the City—Amendment to the Interim Statute including map of the Central Zone & Agreement on Mostar from Rome of 18 February 1996', EUAM, 1996.

Court of Auditors, 'Special Report No 2/96 concerning the accounts of the Administrator & the EUAM', *Official Journal of the European Communities*, C287, Volume 39, 30 September 1996.

Internal Papers

'Ideas on Future Political Arrangements of Mostar Municipality'. Note from J. R. Yarwood to Chief of Staff for Administrator, 10 November 1994.

Proposal for a Mostar Reconstruction Bank. Memorandum from J. R. Yarwood to Chief of Staff and Director of Finance and Taxes, 10 February 1995.

Housing Repair Strategy 1995/96. Report prepared by J. R. Yarwood, 10 February 1995.

Construction Industry Development Plan. Report prepared by J. R. Yarwood, February 1995.

Strategy for EU Administration of Mostar. Paper approved on 13 May 1995.

All Mostar Urban Structure Plan—Terms of Reference. Attached to contract dated 12 October 1995.

'Report Defining a Boundary for a Central Administrative District using Technical Criteria'. Report and memorandum dated 17 January 1996 from J. R. Yarwood and F. Aiello to Administrator. Accompanied by map and tables.

Map drawn by Hans Koschnick recording his counter-proposal for a central district (not dated).

Political Report (July 1994 to December 1996) prepared by Sir Martin Garrod. EUAM, 31 January 1998.

1 Map of Central Mostar (Crown Copyright 1996)

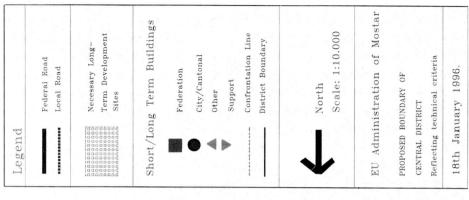

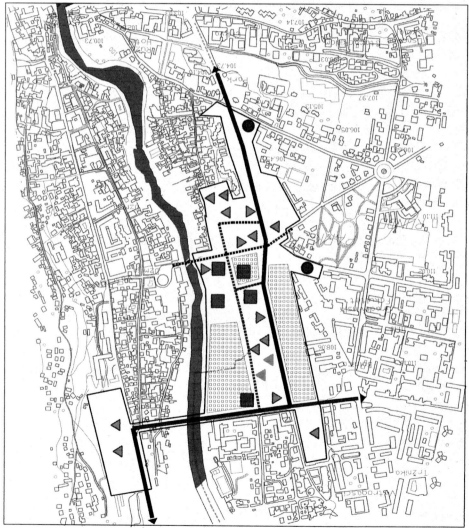

2 Map of Proposal for Central District, including the boundary, prepared by the author, Francesco Aiello and planning staff

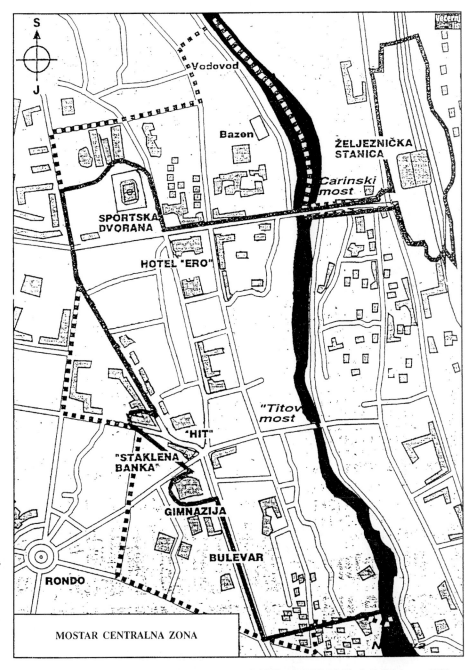

MOSTAR CENTRALNA ZONA

████████   ROME AGREEMENT of 18 February, 1996

3 Map of Central District boundary agreed at the Rome conference of 18 February 1996 (published in the Official Gazette of the City of Mostar, 20 February 1996)

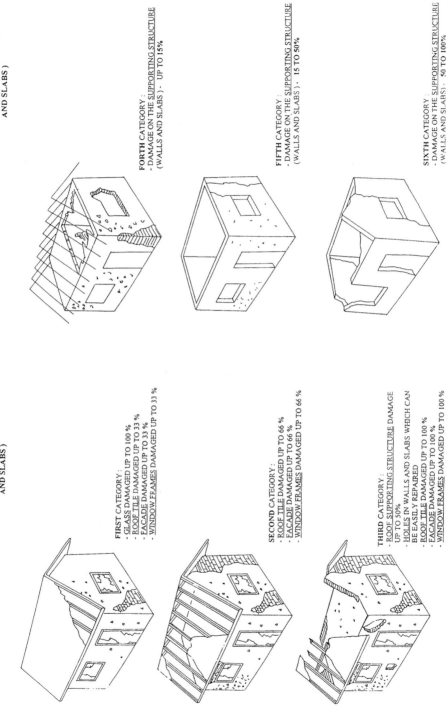

THREE CATEGORIES WITHOUT DAMAGE
ON THE SUPPORTING STRUCTURE (WALLS
AND SLABS)

FIRST CATEGORY:
- GLASS DAMAGED UP TO 100 %
- ROOF TILE DAMAGED UP TO 33 %
- FACADE DAMAGED UP TO 33 %
- WINDOW FRAMES DAMAGED UP TO 33 %

SECOND CATEGORY:
- ROOF TILE DAMAGED UP TO 66 %
- FACADE DAMAGED UP TO 66 %
- WINDOW FRAMES DAMAGED UP TO 66 %

THIRD CATEGORY:
- ROOF SUPPORTING STRUCTURE DAMAGE
  UP TO 50%
- HOLES IN WALLS AND SLABS WHICH CAN
  BE EASILY REPAIRED
- ROOF TILE DAMAGED UP TO 100 %
- FACADE DAMAGED UP TO 100 %
- WINDOW FRAMES DAMAGED UP TO 100 %

THREE CATEGORIES WITH DAMAGE
ON THE SUPPORTING STRUCTURE (WALLS
AND SLABS)

FORTH CATEGORY:
- DAMAGE ON THE SUPPORTING STRUCTURE
  (WALLS AND SLABS) - UP TO 15%

FIFTH CATEGORY:
- DAMAGE ON THE SUPPORTING STRUCTURE
  (WALLS AND SLABS) - 15 TO 50%

SIXTH CATEGORY:
- DAMAGE ON THE SUPPORTING STRUCTURE
  (WALLS AND SLABS) - 50 TO 100%

4 Graphic definition of six damage categories used in the survey of damage. Categories one and two are light damage, three and four medium and five and six heavy damage.

5 View of the Old Bridge from the south, as it appeared in the late 1980s

6 View of the Old Bridge from the south in 1997. The temporary suspension bridge can be seen, and in the foreground are stones recovered from the river bed

7 View northwards from the temporary replacement of the Old Bridge. To the right of the river, the minaret of Koski Mehmet Paša mosque was felled by a shell

8 Ruined buildings on the confrontation line between Alexa Šantića Street and the River Neretva

9 View along Šantića Street, looking north. This heavily damaged street was on the confrontation line

10 View from the Hotel Ero over gutted housing on Šantića Street. The roofs and floors are gone. Gables and chimneys are still standing. Serb artillery was on Podveledže hill in the background in the early months of the mandate

11 A typical heavily damaged two-storey building on the north side of Mostarskog Bataljona Street, near Hit Square

12 Works in progress to stabilise, clean and protect a heavily damaged three-storey building on Maršala Tita Street next to Lučki Bridge

13 The Hotel Neretva viewed from Musala Square, after the initial cleaning of rubble. The interior is gutted and the pitched roof wholly destroyed

14 Musala Square, with the old Music School on the right. To the left (background) is the Razvitak Building, a nine-storey block of apartments, totally gutted. It was later demolished

15 The Music School after stabilisation

16 The Prostor Building (Vakufski Dvor): most of the façade collapsed into the street, and the roof as well as internal walls and floors had fallen into the interior

17 The Cadastral Institute was also totally gutted and some of the façade collapsed

18 The Old Privredna Bank building at Hit Square. Most of the reinforced concrete was standing, but the two left hand bays had collapsed into a big pile of rubble. Columns and floors were hanging down, attached only by the reinforcing bars

19 A side view of the Old Privredna Bank, with the Borovo Building on the left, prior to demolition and cleaning

20 A typical building in the Ottoman Bazaar, after cleaning. Protection was given to the roof by plastic sheeting

21 Stabile structure to prevent collapse of arched entry to the Old Bridge

22 Cleaning of rubble from the interior of the Halebinovka Tower (a fortification of the Old Bridge) and also works to protect from further decay

23 Entrance to Ottoman han in the old town: the roof and interior are gutted

24 Old house, with roof and top storey collapsed: Austrian period, but located in the old town, Onesčukova

25 Typical medium destroyed house in the Brankovac area

26 Typical medium destroyed house in the Cernica area

27 Typical heavily destroyed houses in Donja Mahala; only external walls remain. In the background, the freshly tiled roofs of repaired houses can be seen

28 The Public Health Institute, showing sandbags and other improvised fortifications typical of Mostar during the wars

29 The Hit Department Store (which was on the confrontation line) prior to demolition

30 The Revija Building, an apartment block on Mostarskog Bataljona Street, after repair. It was so heavily damaged that only the reinforced concrete frame remained

31 Apartment block known as No. 4 Šantića Street, after repair. This was just as heavily damaged as the Revija Building

32 The Bejrut Building after repair. This apartment block (located next to the Bus Station) was badly damaged, but remained partially inhabited throughout the wars

33 The apartment blocks at 82/86 Maršala Tita Street (viewed from Brace Fejice Street) after repair. They, too, were badly damaged by shells and fire

34 The Soliter Tower, a block of apartments in Zalik, after repair. The top half of the building was pierced by shells and completely burned out

35 The Hotel Bristol after repair. After shelling, only the reinforced concrete frame remained. This was repaired as a hostel for returning experts, such as doctors and engineers

36 The main Railway Station, after repair

37 The Court building, Kolodvorska Street, after repair. This fine neo-classical structure was heavily damaged and was repaired to high standards in order to restart the justice system

38 The Headquarters of the United Police Force of Mostar after repair. Before the wars it had been the offices of a building company and was heavily destroyed

39 The New Dom Zdravlja (Health Centre) built to provide primary care. It is located on the confrontation line. The Old Dom Zdravlja, built in 1935 (architect, Drago Ibler) was heavily damaged but still stands nearby

40 'South Camp' Hospital was created by converting a heavily damaged former military building. Full medical equipment was provided

41 Brankovac Paediatric and Obstetric Hospital involved repair of an existing, damaged clinic, but this was extended by adding an additional storey and a rear wing. Full medical equipment was provided

42 A typical local clinic (or 'ambulanta'); this one is at Buna. Some clinics were repaired and some built new (as necessary)

43 The new EUAM Technical Training Centre (street frontage) after repair

44 The house on the left has been re-roofed and repaired. The house on the right is gutted, but materials for its repair can be seen stacked on site

45 This house was gutted, but two rooms (on the right) were fully repaired. More than this could not be afforded

46 Repair of the two houses on the left is complete, but repair to the house in the middle is not yet finished. Damaged houses can be seen on the right

47 Drilling for new wells in east Mostar

48 Testing water flow from the newly drilled wells

49 Mr Hans Koschnick, the EU Administrator of Mostar

50 HE Klaus Metscher, the Diplomatic Adviser (and also Mr Koschnick's Deputy). HE Costas Zepos, the EUAM Ombudsman, is on the left of the photograph

51 HE Bo Kaelfors, Refugee Adviser (left), talking to Sir Martin Garrod, Chief of Staff

52 Douglas Houston (right) and John Adlam (centre) of the UK Overseas Development Administration, with Sir Martin Garrod (left) on Kujundžiluk Street, with the remains of the Old Bridge in the background

53 A group photograph of some Reconstruction Department staff in the office of the housing section

54 Andreas Seebacher, a member of the engineering staff of Technisches Hilfswerk

55 Before leaving for Mostar, the author is briefed by Lady Chalker, Minister of Overseas Development at the time

56 Delivery of building materials to a typical site. A delivery lorry belonging to THW can be seen. The house on the left has already been re-roofed and shell holes have been bricked up

57 The THW Materials Warehouse in the old Tobacco Factory, east Mostar. A lorry has just been loaded

58 Material delivery and unloading in a narrow street typical of the old town

59 The Hotel Ero in summer 1994. A street barricade can be seen in the foreground

60 Some West European policemen gathering outside the Reconstruction Department office to protect it in the event of the February 1996 riot spreading